CHRISTIANITY ON THE FRONTIER

by

JOHN A. MACKAY
*President of Princeton
Theological Seminary*

WIPF & STOCK · Eugene, Oregon

Wipf and Stock Publishers
199 W 8th Ave, Suite 3
Eugene, OR 97401

Christianity on the Frontier
By Mackay, John A.
Copyright © 1950 by Mackay, John A. All rights reserved.
Literary Agent: John Mackay Metzger
Softcover ISBN-13: 979-8-3852-4243-6
Hardcover ISBN-13: 979-8-3852-4244-3
eBook ISBN-13: 979-8-3852-4245-0
Publication date 1/6/2025
Previously published by The Macmillan Company, 1950

This edition is a scanned facsimile of the original edition published in 1950.

DEDICATED

To my co-workers on *Theology Today*

FOREWORD

THE ESSAYS THAT MAKE UP THIS BOOK WERE written at different times and in diverse circumstances during the last six years. Most of them were first printed as editorials in the theological quarterly *Theology Today*.

Two have appeared elsewhere. The long essay on Protestantism, with which Part Two begins, is taken from a volume entitled *The Great Religions of the Modern World*, published by the Princeton University Press. *The Holy Spirit in Proclamation* was given as an address at a meeting of the International Missionary Council held at Whitby, Canada, in July 1947, and subsequently published in a book edited by the Reverend Charles W. Ranson, entitled *Renewal and Advance*. For their courteous permission to incorporate these two studies in the present volume, grateful thanks are tendered, in the first instance to the Princeton University Press and Oxford University Press and, in the second, to the International Missionary Council.

As I have read over again these essays, which were selected and arranged in their present order by the Lutterworth Press, with the approval of the Macmillan Company, I have become conscious of several things. A few basic ideas run through them all. These ideas which have seemed to me important are presented in varying connections and appear in a variety of forms. A great concern and a great conviction give unity to the whole.

The *concern* is this: the Christian Church and all Christians everywhere should live a "frontier" life. They should be in that place where Life's most crucial issues await a Christian decision; they should be there too where Life presents new areas to be possessed in the name of Christ. For the "frontier" is a place of tension, as in the traditional European meaning of the term; it is also "the hitherside of new land", the place beyond which lies unoccupied territory, as in the familiar American meaning.

The *conviction* is that Jesus Christ, the Word of God Incarnate, shall triumph in history, and not merely beyond history.

Some of the papers that follow were written while the War was still raging, others since the "Peace" has come. Not one of them was looked at again until all were sent me to be re-read in proof in their present setting. Such repetitions therefore, in allusion or concept, in emphasis or expression, as the reader may find them to contain I ask him to forgive. Perchance there is a place for the repetitions of faith in a time marked by the repetition of folly.

This book, whose origin and structure have thus been so casual, may be regarded in a certain sense as the third member in an undesigned trilogy. In *A Preface to Christian Theology* I tried to say: Leave the Balcony for the Road. *Heritage and Destiny* sought to embody the thought: The Road to Tomorrow leads through Yesterday. The burden of this little tome might be stated thus: Take the Road to the Frontier.

January, 1950   J.A.M.

Contents

PART ONE

	Page
1. GOD HAS SPOKEN	13
2. THE HOLY SPIRIT IN PROCLAMATION	22
3. LET THE CHURCH LIVE ON THE FRONTIER	41
4. THE PERIL OF A VACUUM	53
5. THE CRUCIAL ALTERNATIVES	62
6. FIRE OR FIRE	75
7. THE CONTRIBUTION OF THE REFORMED CHURCHES TO CHRISTIAN DOCTRINE	86

PART TWO

8. PROTESTANTISM	97
9. AS REGARDS FREEDOM OF RELIGION	143
10. A THEOLOGICAL MEDITATION ON LATIN AMERICA	153
11. MEXICAN MUSINGS	169
12. THOUGHTS ON TRUTH AND UNITY	177
13. THE NEXT STEPS	189
14. THE END IS THE BEGINNING	198

PART ONE

1

GOD HAS SPOKEN

THE BOOK THAT MEN MOST NEED TO STUDY IS THE book of which they know little and understand less. That book is the Bible. The Bible, it is true, occupies a unique position among the books of the world. It is, we are told, literature's greatest monument, the book that circulates most widely, that speaks its message in a thousand tongues. All this is true. Yet, amid the plaudits that greet the Bible when its name is mentioned, there is a sobering fact that tempers exultation: the Book of books is the great unknown among its kind. To make the Bible known by the people of to-day is the supreme cultural and religious task of our time.

What is the Bible essentially? It is the record of God's revelation to mankind, the abiding witness to the fact that He has spoken. *God has spoken.* This is the message of the Bible. There is a word from the Lord, an authoritative account of His relations to the world and to man. The eternal silence has been broken. Light has shone upon the mystery of man's life. A divine answer has been given to the problem of his sin. The hidden God has become manifest in a new order of life. The one stupendous fact with which the Bible deals is that God has spoken by saving deeds and enlightening words. The Book is the record of His self-communication at different times and through diverse agents. It is thereby, in a wholly unique sense, the Word of God.

How God Has Spoken

But how has God spoken? In nature, in the heart of man, and in the general religious history of mankind, witness is borne to the godhead of the Creator. But in the history of the Hebrew people God revealed Himself in a unique manner as the living, speaking, and redeeming God. He made Himself known through saving acts and through men who interpreted His ways and purposes.

The Bible is, in particular, a record of encounters which specific individuals had with God, whereby He revealed Himself in their experience and understanding of Him. Time and again God is described as " the God of Abraham, the God of Isaac, and the God of Jacob ". The lives of these men He wove into an historical redemptive pattern, making them the representative types of men in whose lives He still works and speaks. To understand what this means is crucial to our understanding of the Bible.

The designation of God in the Bible as the " God of Israel " bears witness to the fact that in the life-history of a race which bore the name of Jacob, their ancestor, He revealed Himself in a way that became significant for them and, through them, for mankind. God's revelation through Israel was not due to the fact that this people was exceptionally gifted in a religious sense. Indeed, the religious history of the Hebrew people from the days of Jacob and his sons, the founders of the Twelve Tribes of Israel, to the time when Israel disappeared as a nation is, in many respects, a sordid tale. But by great redemptive acts, by a long process of hard discipline, and through the leadership of men who did His bidding and interpreted His purposes, God formed a race of people through whom His purposes were both revealed and carried forward in history.

Most significant as God's interpreters among all the members of the Hebrew people are the prophets from Moses to John the Baptist. It is impossible to understand or to do justice to the Old Testament unless it is recognized that in all its parts it bears witness to the inspiration and insight of the Prophets. The lives and, in some cases, the writings, of these unique figures reveal the meaning of encounter with God. God, we read, " came " to them; He " took " them. They " saw " Him; they " heard " Him. They received insight into God. They spoke about Israel's God as the God of the whole earth, the one and only God. Under the inspiration of the same Spirit that brooded over chaos and made an ordered universe, they set God's redemptive purpose for Israel and the world within the majestic framework of creation. They set it also in the living stream of world history. Taking objects and practices which the Hebrews had derived from other nations and the influence of other religions, they infused into these new meaning, and made them an integral part of the religion of Israel. Many objects and practices, for example, which were connected with the symbolism and ritual of the tabernacle and the temple, became, despite their lowly and foreign origin, types of holy mysteries, and patterns of holy living.

In a supreme and absolute sense God revealed Himself as the God of a unique person, Jesus Christ. The most significant name by which He is known in the Bible is " the God and Father of our Lord Jesus Christ ". In the fullness of time and at the centre of history a Man appeared. In Him were fulfilled the longings of Israel for a Messiah. In Him also received fulfilment the predictions of the prophets regarding a Deliverer in whom God's purpose for mankind would find its focal expression and from whom would emanate light and power to make God and His purpose fully manifest. The coming of the Christ is the supreme event to which the Old Testament looks forward.

Of Jesus Christ, the Word of God become flesh, it can be said that He revealed to the world what God is and what man should be. His life was not a casual appearance in history, for God had *sent* Him. His character was not a solitary expression of ideal goodness, for God was *like* Him. His life purpose, which led Him to a cross, was not a vain beating against a meaningless or hostile universe, for God was *in* Him. The Resurrection was the proof that He was truly the Word of God Incarnate. It was also the pledge that no word that He had spoken would fall to the ground. For God, who had spoken through the prophets, had now spoken in a Son.

The men and women who recognized Jesus as the Messiah of Israel and believed in Him as the Christ of God, became a new community. This community was brought into being and indwelt by the same Holy Spirit who had created the world, inspired the prophets, and given Jesus Christ to mankind. It became the new, the spiritual, Israel, the Body of Jesus Christ, the organ of His redemptive will in history. In the course of the years, and under the inspiration of the same Spirit, the Church formed the Canon of Holy Scripture. In and through the Church and its history, God still guides Christians into an ever larger understanding of His redemptive purpose centring in Jesus Christ. The Holy Spirit awakens in the hearts of Christian believers, members of the Body of Christ, the filial attitude towards God which leads them to say " Father ". He convinces them also of the essential truth of Holy Scripture by the witness of His own presence in their hearts.

What God Has Said

What is it that God has said? The Gospel, the Good News, contained in the Old Testament and in the New, regarding God's gracious purpose for mankind, is the content of the Bible message. In the study of this content the Bible must be understood in its own light. Its categories and terms are native, and not alien, to itself. No part of it can be understood or interpreted in isolation from the other parts, but only in relation to the whole. Only a method of study which starts from Jesus Christ, in whom the fullness of God and His purpose became manifest and which uses Him as the supreme key and clue to an interpretation of Scripture, can make the central meaning of the Bible plain. Only by such a method can the substance of God's self-disclosure be apprehended and its progressive character become clear. Only in this way, too, can the error be avoided of perpetuating practices which were valid at an earlier stage in God's dealing with men, before His full purpose became manifest in Christ. In studying any part of the Bible it is necessary that everything shall be judged with full attention to the significance of Christ's own words, " Ye have heard that it was said by men of old times . . . but I say unto you . . ." Nothing is more unbiblical, nor can anything be more perilous, than to take certain words and commands of God out of their proper context in the Bible and attempt to give them permanent and independent validity.

The deepest note in the Bible is the affirmation of a spiritual unity closely related to the unveiling of God and His gracious purpose in Christ. A unity, like the unity of a musical harmony, underlies the whole. This harmony has an exultant quality. The world of man which came to the birth in music, when " the morning stars sang together and all the sons of God shouted for joy ", will end in a redemptive harmony. Notes of music will celebrate the achievement of redemption by him who redeems men to God from " every tribe and people and tongue and nation ".

The education of the chosen people was basically a training in the unity of God and His purpose. God, the Lord, being one God, the law of life is one law. True human living consists in obedience to the will of God. Accordingly, " The fear of the Lord is the beginning of wisdom ". But before this holy fear is engendered and wisdom obtained, each human heart must be " united " in its secret places.

Unity is established between God and His people by a covenant, whereby they become God's " portion " and He becomes their "portion", their inheritance. The ultimate goal of this community of life and purpose between God and His covenant-people is, according to the Old Testament, that the nations of mankind should be blessed through Israel and become one in the God of Israel.

But before this redemptive unity can be achieved in history, there must appear in Israel the Suffering Servant, who, on account of the sins of his people and of all people, would be bruised and broken and rejected by men, in order that he might see the travail of his soul and constitute a new and united family of God from among all the nations of mankind. Therefore, the supreme unity is revealed in Jesus Christ, the Son of God, who was perfectly one with the Father. The unity of character and will between Jesus Christ and His Father led Him to the Cross. The Cross of Christ is the supreme revelation of human sin. It is also the supreme manifestation of God's judgment upon sin and of His redeeming love whereby He creates new men in Christ.

The unity achieved in the reconciliation between man and God in the Cross of Jesus Christ led to the establishment of a new unity in the relations between man and man in human society. Elements in society and history between which no true partnership had hitherto existed became one. Jews and Gentiles, masters and servants, men and women, cultured and unlettered, all became one in Christ as members of His Body, the Church. Through the Church as the Body of Christ, God's will would be made known and done among men; His Kingdom would come; His will would be "done upon earth as it is in heaven".

Why God Has Spoken

But why should God have spoken? Unless God had revealed Himself and His will, men could never have known Him or His purpose. According to the Bible, it was the deep rift in human nature and the expression of man's rebellious will against his Maker that led to the self-disclosure of God, the record of which is contained in the Bible. The purpose of the divine revelation being, therefore, redemptive in character, the Bible must never be regarded merely as a Book which supplies information. It is not interested in telling about nature as such, or even about God as such, or about the future of the world as such. Much harm has been done in the history of civilization and within the Christian Church by regarding the Bible as a store-house of wisdom on matters which do not concern it. Upon many important matters God has left men to make their own investigations and come to their own conclusions. The truth revealed in the Bible is redemptive truth. It is truth in order to goodness. It opens up to men how they may be redeemed unto goodness of life, unto consecration to the will of God, in the time and place and circumstances in which they find themselves. That being so, they only can understand the Bible and are capable of interpreting it who, feeling their need of redemption, come to its pages in search of God's answer to the problem of their sin and their unsatisfied yearning. To hear the Word of God speak to us through these sacred pages means to recognize that what God desires is man's response in repentance and faith and to take action accordingly. Only when God is obeyed is He truly known.

Recognizing, therefore, that the Bible is a book about redemption which is to be studied in the perspective of redemption and in the light of that central redemptive figure, Jesus Christ, we are brought into a truly Biblical attitude toward the nature of God's self-disclosure. We give up the attempt to understand the Bible by merely dissecting its documents into parts. We do not lose time in the vain, unbiblical effort to make the Bible a text-book in matters in which God did not intend it to be authoritative. But in all matters pertaining to our knowledge of God, the salvation of the soul, the ordering of human society, the upbuilding of the Christian Church, the coming of God's Kingdom, it is in and through the Bible that God speaks His word of command and grace.

There is a sense, indeed, in which the Bible may be described as a very direct and intimate letter to " whom it may concern ". In its ultimate meaning, beyond all questions about authors and documents, about the origin and development of many ideas and practices contained in the Record, it is a letter from God to mankind. By its diffusion among all nations and the individual challenge of the truth it conveys, this book carries upon it the name and address of every people and person to whom it comes. To each of these it comes not as a book about religion, not even as a book about God. It comes rather as a very intimate and personal communication to all men, corporately and individually, to hear and obey the Word which the living God addresses to them.

2

THE HOLY SPIRIT IN PROCLAMATION

ATTENTION NEEDS TO BE DRAWN INCREASINGLY to the fact that in the Christian religion there is a "given Word". It is the task of Christians to articulate that Word in speech appropriate to its nature, and which shall be both intelligible and arresting to those who in each succeeding generation listen to it. But the Word of God is given and articulated that it may be proclaimed. My aim in this study is to consider the place of the Holy Spirit in the proclamation of the Word.

The Holy Spirit is represented in the Bible as the agent of God's will in word and deed. In both the Old Testament and the New, the Spirit is described under the symbolical imagery of a "wind", a "breath". The characteristic word in the Old Testament is *ruach*; in the New it is *pneuma*. The Hebrew and Greek terms are synonymous. When we take into account the references to the Spirit in the Bible as a whole we find that He may be defined, or at least described, as "God in action in human life". It is important to observe that this Divine activity expressed by the presence of the Spirit is invasive rather than pervasive. The Spirit enters life from the outside. When He comes, He fills and controls life utterly, but He does so, not as an inherently immanent Presence but rather as a transcendent Presence who invades the human soul or a human situation on a special divine mission.

When we consider the activity of the Spirit in relation to the world and to man we discover that, both in the order of nature and in the order of redemption, His presence brings into play both the wisdom and the power of God. When Creation was in process and there was nothing but a vast void, the Spirit of God brooded like a bird over the abyss. " The Spirit of God was brooding upon the face of the waters " (Gen. 1 : 2). When in Ezekiel's vision the dry bones in the valley had come together and the skeletons were covered with flesh and sinew, the breath, in response to the prophetic word uttered at God's command, came from the four winds and the dead " lived, and stood up upon their feet, an exceeding great army " (Ezekiel 37 : 1–10). Jesus, we read, came out of the wilderness in the power of the Spirit, who had anointed Him at His baptism; and all His mighty works were wrought through the Spirit. We learn that it was the Spirit of God who gave special insight to the men who designed and furnished the Tabernacle. The same Spirit endued the prophets with wisdom to speak God's message. The Lord Jesus Christ applied to Himself the prophecy in Isaiah which speaks of One who is to come. " The Spirit of the Lord is upon me; because he hath anointed me to preach the gospel to the poor ", etc. (Isaiah 61 : 1–3; Luke 4 : 18, 19). It was the same Holy Spirit, moreover, who after Christ's departure was " to take of the things of Christ and reveal them " to the disciples. He, the "Spirit of truth", was to lead the followers of Jesus "into all truth".

I

The rôle of the Holy Spirit in the proclamation of the Gospel would appear to be threefold. First: *It is the Holy Spirit who provides the message.* What is the Gospel message, "the given Word", "the glad tidings"? In simplest terms it is this: God in Jesus Christ has wrought complete salvation for man. Because of something that God has done to which the Christian Church must bear witness, man can be "saved". God's image can be restored upon him so that he becomes God-like. His life becomes God-centred and thus truly human. "Saved" men become partakers of eternal life, of God's own nature; in the deepest sense, they become "sons of God".

Christian truth, especially the Word of the Gospel, is not timeless truth about God. It is truth that *became*. The Christian message, the message of the good news about God which constitutes the core of the Gospel, is not so much good news about what God is eternally, as it is good news about something done by God in time which has eternal significance. The Holy Spirit is historically related to the Christian message in three important ways.

(a) The Spirit was present as a decisive factor in the redemptive events themselves. He "overshadowed" the Virgin Mary so that she conceived of the Holy Ghost. In the form of a dove He descended upon the head of Jesus as He was being baptized by John in the Jordan river and equipped

Him for His public ministry. In the power of the Spirit Jesus preached and healed and did His mighty works. " Through the eternal Spirit He offered Himself without spot to God" (Heb. 9: 14). Through the power of the Spirit, He rose again from the dead. The descent of the Holy Spirit at Pentecost, in accordance with the promise of Jesus, empowered the apostles to do their work and brought into being the Christian Church, which is the "fellowship of the Spirit", that is, the fellowship created by the Spirit. The Christian Church is itself an event whose glorious reality is both the fruit of the Gospel and an integral part of the Gospel; for when the Church is true to its nature, it is an abiding witness to the reality of the glad tidings.

(*b*) It is the Holy Spirit, moreover, who provides an authoritative interpretation of the Christian message. The Biblical writers who wrote about Christ and the Gospel were under the Spirit's influence in their writing. So, too, was the Church in the formation of the Biblical canon. While we reject the suggestion of anything mechanical or magical in the literary activity of the Biblical authors, or in the men who selected some writings to form the Biblical record and rejected others, we have in the Bible not merely an account of redemptive events; we have, with varying emphasis, an inspired, authoritative interpretation of those events. The Bible is a personal witness to the redemptive working of God on man's behalf. It is something much more than literature's greatest monument of religious thought. It is something very much more than the unique and exclusive source of first-hand information regarding God's redemptive activity in history. It is more even than an authoritative source book for the formulation of Christian doctrine. It is, above all, the unique and permanent medium of communication between God and man. Here God speaks to man and here man, listening to God and making the decision which God asks him to make, becomes aware that he is in the presence of "invincible truth". Through the testimony of the Holy Spirit in his heart man knows that God is speaking to him in the words of the Bible. Just as no mechanical or magical view of inspiration does justice to the majestic reality of the fact that God has spoken, so no scholastic view of Revelation, which reduces it to the revelation of propositions, does justice in any way to the luminous, soul-warming and soul-transforming presence of God in His Word. It is at this point that the Evangelical view of the Bible goes far beyond the Roman Catholic view. The Roman Catholic finds truth about God in the Bible; the Evangelical believer finds God Himself in the Bible. There, in the witness borne to Jesus Christ, God meets him in life's supreme encounter and continues to commune with him in life's supreme fellowship. That is the reason why the Evangelical Christian lives upon the Bible, from which he derives daily sustenance. Its place can never be taken in his experience, either by the recital of credal statements or by the devout participation in sacramental rites.

(c) But the Spirit is related to the Christian message in still another way. His abiding presence in the Christian Church since Pentecost has been manifested in the great Confessional statements of faith which proclaim the Church's unswerving loyalty to Jesus

Christ, and which continue to be sources of inspiration and rallying centres for unity. While, of course, the great Christian creeds can only be regarded as human documents without any claim to infallibility, there run through them statements of truths which bear the marks of the Spirit's guidance and inspiration. While the marks of human finitude and of historical contingency are imprinted upon them all, they contain flashes of truth, depths of insight, and statements of faith which have abiding significance for the Christian Church. Not for one moment can we accept the idea that the task of formulating Christian truth in dogmatic concepts has all to be done over again. While it is true that each great Confessional statement was directed towards some heresy or another, over against which the attempt was made to formulate with crystalline clarity the Biblical truth, there is no reason to suppose that these formulations do not admit us into a doctrinal understanding of abiding value. The creeds of the undivided Church and the Reformation Confessions will continue to be an enduring part of the Church's heritage of thought. When, for example, the doctrine of the Universal Priesthood of Believers was formulated, conceptual form was given to a truth that is inherent in the Christian religion and which constitutes an integral part of divine revelation. So, too, the doctrine of the Unmediated Lordship of Jesus Christ, which constitutes the basis of a doctrine of Evangelical catholicity, links itself to the ancient saying, "where Christ is there is the Church"; because where Christ is there will be manifest in rich abundance the fruits of the Holy Spirit in thought and life and action. We cannot affirm, " I believe in the Holy Ghost ", without believing in a very real sense that the Spirit has been leading the Church into all truth; provided always that the Church has been open to His inspiration and guidance, and has been willing to walk obediently in the ways of Christ and according to His mind.

II

In the second place: *It is the Holy Spirit who equips the messengers of the Word.* They are " the Lord's messengers in the Lord's message ". The same Spirit who provides the Word and leads a human life to accept it, equips that life for the special service of bearing witness to the Christian truth. The messenger of the Word is anointed with the Holy Ghost. It is his privilege and obligation to be " filled with the Spirit ".

How does the Spirit equip the Gospel herald that he may proclaim his message with warmth and insight, with heat and light?

Evangelical unction is not to be confused with aesthetic appreciation. Aesthetic appreciation is that natural admiration which is awakened in a person by the emotional values that are implicit in the Christian revelation, and which it is the function of art to make visible in enthralling artistic forms, through colour, sound and speech. It is much more than the reverence that is awakened in a man when he finds himself in the presence of the supreme moral imperative to love God and his neighbour. It is something very much more than the logical conclusion which thought reaches after it has been led by discursive reasoning to accept the validity of the Christian Faith. Evangelical unction means to be seized, grasped, possessed by the Word. It is to be weighted with a burden which one must deliver with a passionate sense of mission. It is to experience a fire within one, a burning heart, which breaks forth into passionate speech. It is an " apostolic madness " which in certain epochs and occasions bursts the bounds of conventional communication and the accepted proprieties of address. It is a belt which girds and braces the mind to proclaim the truth at a time when others are pursuing it like a butterfly or a bird. It is to feel, as Paul felt when he said, " Woe is me if I preach not the Gospel "; as the earlier apostles felt when they replied to those who had arraigned them and commanded them to keep silent, " We cannot but speak the things which we have seen and heard ". It is the spiritual endowment which, down through the Christian ages, has created spirits of flame, making them the centre of great movements of spiritual revival. It is an " unction from the Holy One ", with which not only great leaders of the Church but multitudes of simple people have been endued. But all of those people, whatever their culture or estate, were passionate witnesses to the redeeming Word of God and to the grace of the Lord Jesus Christ, proclaiming that Word and exemplifying that grace in every situation in which they found themselves.

This Evangelical unction which is the birthright of all believers in Jesus Christ, and which all should possess and manifest, is one of the great lacks, as it is one of the great needs, of the Christian Church in our time. Spiritual passion in the proclamation of the Gospel is the only way in which the Gospel, being what it is, can be worthily proclaimed. Not only so, but only those things that are proclaimed in burning speech can make the slightest impression upon a world which is being dominated more and more by passionate crusaders of one kind or another. It is a striking fact that the two leading poets in the English tongue to-day, T. S. Eliot, an American who spends most of his time in England, and W. H. Auden, an Englishman who spends most of his time in America, both sense the need of passion in the representatives of religion, if religious truth is to make its way among the crusading slogans that compete for human attention in this revolutionary age. Yeats had said,

> The best lack all conviction,
> And the worst are full of passionate intensity.

By this he meant that those people whom, by their loyalty to traditional ways, we have come to regard as the best representatives of our culture, are entirely lacking in strong ideas which they would be willing to die for, whereas folk regarded as "reds" and upstarts are people of burning passion.

> Ruffle the perfect manners of the frozen heart,
> And once again compel it to be awkward and alive.[1]

Here Auden is committed to the idea that the uncouthness of real life is to be preferred to the manifestations of aesthetic death. T. S. Eliot, on the other hand, if we interpret him aright, sees the issue as one between the fire generated by a purely sensate expression of life and the purifying fire of the Spirit.

[1] *Commentary,* Collected Works.

> The only hope, or else despair
> Lies in the choice of pyre or pyre
> To be redeemed from fire by fire.
>
> . . . .
>
> We only live, only suspire,
> Consumed by either fire or fire.[1]

It must be the Spirit of God or the demonic spirits; there is no real alternative. Conviction that centres in God, passion that is inspired by God, can alone offset the passion and conviction engendered by the demonic, that is, by finite realities which become gods in the minds and hearts of men.

What splendid conviction and passion have marked the lives of the devotees of Christianity's rivals in the thought and life of these last times! What was sublimer than the biological devotion of young Nazis to their cause and leader? Like hounds that sniff the morning breeze and strain at the leash, like pedigree steeds that await the crack of the whip or the blare of the trumpet to start out on the hunt, they awaited their master's voice that sent them headlong on their way. In the bondage of unquestioning loyalty, they exulted in a liberating freedom.

But, thank God, men and women filled with the Holy Spirit have attained a conviction and possessed a passion surer and purer than anything ever achieved by Nazi or secular crusader. It is precisely this " unction from the Holy One " that we need. But how terrible it is to think that in these last times strong conviction and burning passion have not been popular in Christian circles! It is not necessary that conviction and passion should express themselves in

[1] *Little Gidding*, Faber and Faber.

the objectionable form which we associate only with fanatics. A friend from China told me some time ago that the reason why the Communists have been able to make such headway in that great republic is that, when they mingle in the market-place with others, they " gossip about their faith ". For Christians filled with the Spirit it becomes the most natural thing in the world to proclaim their Christian faith by word and by deed, wherever the opportunity offers. If unction is present a way will be found to pass on the Christian truth in a manner which, so far from being offensive, will find the most natural and effective point of contact with all people and circumstances. It is time, therefore, in the name of Christ and in the power of the Spirit, to react against that attitude of mind which " sterilizes fanaticism at the cost of extinguishing faith ".

The Holy Spirit, however, gives not only unction but also understanding to the Christian messenger. He receives light as well as heat from the Spirit; otherwise his enthusiasm would be indistinguishable from that of the fanatic. But the Holy Spirit takes the things of Christ and reveals them unto us. That is the great interpretative function of the Spirit, to make Jesus Christ not only real to us so that He fills and satisfies our whole emotional nature, but also luminous and intelligible to us, so that we come to relate Him to every problem of thought and every issue of life. The Incarnate Word of God illumines the understanding of those who proclaim the Gospel and seek to apply it. True Christian preaching inspired by the Holy Spirit is always Christo-centric. It lives, moves, and has its being in Christ. The moment

Christian preaching ceases to be Christo-centric it becomes sub-Christian. Every aspect of the reality of Christ must find its place in proclamation; His person and His teaching, the " mighty works " which He did, and the still mightier work which God did in and through Him.

For that reason Christian preaching inspired by the Spirit must be inescapably doctrinal. There are no truths that are so luminous, and none that have more piercing and healing relevance to the contemporary situation, than the great Christian doctrines about God and man. When the mind of the Christian messenger, under the influence of the Spirit, broods upon the Christian truth as it centres in Christ and interprets it in terms of his redemptive experience of Christ he achieves an insight into human reality far superior to that of any psychologist, sociologist, political scientist or statesman who thinks about men and the world of men without the light of Christ. The messenger of the Gospel accepts believingly things which, to the secular mind, are quite incredible; he undertakes hopefully things which are regarded as impossible. He believes the rationally incredible and attempts the humanly impossible. Because of his experience of the Spirit, the whole atmosphere of the supernatural becomes real and natural to the true preacher of the Gospel. When assailed by the paradox

> How could the Eternal do a temporal act,
> The Infinite become a finite fact?

his faith triumphs because he understands the feeling of sin and mortality that gives birth to these other words of the poet—

> Nothing can save us that is possible:
> We who must die demand a miracle.

For him the supernatural is the most truly natural and the rationally incredible the highest reason. When the preacher sees the great Christian truths in all their majesty and his personal experience authenticates their reality; when he flashes them like torches upon the human scene; when he shows men their predicament and tells them how they may be saved with an everlasting salvation; then the great doctrines of the Christian religion take on a musical as well as a luminous character. Christian truth, when worthily proclaimed, is not only a light; it has also a lilt. It illumines the abyss of human need and lights up the whole redemptive purpose of God; but it has also a singing note, because it is personal truth proclaimed by a life that has learned to sing the new song of God. It is this singing note, more than anything else, that is needed in our time. The preaching of the Gospel must resemble the singing of songs at midnight, songs of hope amid the anguish and despair of our age. It is this singing note, these " songs in the night ", that will again become the signal for prison doors to open and for captives' bonds to be loosed, as when Paul and Silas made their prison-house re-echo with their minstrelsy.

But the Spirit does something more. He gives understanding to the messenger with respect to the circumstances and conditions in which he can best discharge his mission. The Spirit not only endues him with a sensitivity as to the words which he should most appropriately speak, especially in crises and unexpected circumstances; He guides him also as to where and among whom his ministry will be most effective. The Spirit " suffers not " one messenger to go into Asia, but He leads another along a desert trail to join himself to a man of Ethiopia who needs his help. The more responsive the messenger is to the guidance of the Spirit, the more fruitful will be his ministry in results, in the same way that his words will be the more luminous and challenging in their appeal.

III

We now come to the third influence of the Holy Spirit in proclamation. *It is the Holy Spirit who makes the Word effective.* What is the aim of all true preaching? It is to achieve through the power of the Spirit that those who hear the Word of truth will be so transformed by it as to become God-like in their lives and God-centred in their living. The end of preaching is the conversion of the hearer into a man of God. It is the Holy Spirit who makes the Word effectual unto salvation. It is He who creates the response in the person who is addressed by the Word. He brings about the great encounter between the soul and Jesus Christ. He disposes the soul both to listen to the Word of Christ and to commit himself to the Saviour who has come to claim its allegiance.

There are two classical statements regarding the work of the Spirit in producing spiritual change which it may be helpful to introduce at this point. One is found in that little compendium of Christian truth upon which some of us were brought up from childhood years, *The Westminster Shorter*

Catechism. I refer to the answer to the question "What is effectual calling?" "Effectual calling is the work of God's Spirit, whereby convincing us of our sin and misery, enlightening our minds in the knowledge of Christ, and renewing our wills, He doth persuade and enable us to embrace Jesus Christ freely offered to us in the Gospel." That is a marvellously true and comprehensive statement of what happens when the Spirit, who gives the Word and gives unction to him who preaches the Word, deals with the heart to which the Word comes. Observe in this marvellous answer what the soul does is not merely to assent to truth about Christ but to embrace Christ Himself as He is presented in the truth.

The other classical statement which I have in mind occurs in a brochure published recently by a Commission of the Church of England and entitled *Towards the Conversion of England*.[1] In the definition of evangelism one seems to detect the master mind of that Christian scholar and saint whose life was so much identified with the ecumenical movement: I mean William Temple. Here is the statement: "To evangelize is so to present Christ Jesus in the power of the Holy Spirit, that men shall come to put their trust in God through Him, to accept Him as their Saviour, and serve Him as their King, in the fellowship of His Church."

Very varied may be the form and circumstances in which the soul, under the influence of the Spirit, responds to Jesus Christ and the great change takes place. Sometimes the Word of Christ comes to the soul in thunderous noise like the battering rams of

[1] The Press and Publications Board of the Church Assembly.

THE HOLY SPIRIT IN PROCLAMATION

Boanerges in John Bunyan's famous allegory, *The Holy War*. The reason is obvious. The soul is so dead, eargate is so insensitive, that the voice of Emmanuel is transmitted through His messengers in the booming sound of siege-artillery. Another described his experience thus: " That voice is round me like a bursting sea." At another time it was like " the drift of pinions ", soft and filmy, against " clay-shuttered doors ". At length the Voice sounds from out the encircling gloom, which, as the soul comes to see, is the shadow cast by the Seeker's hand. But in every case *Someone comes to the soul*, loudly or quietly, according to the soul's state; and before the day is over " 'Tis done; the great transaction's done." Soul and Saviour meet in an everlasting covenant of love.

But what does this involve? The Spirit's work in conversion involves repentance and faith. To repent in a Biblical, evangelical sense means to undergo a total change of outlook. It does not mean a mere feeling of sorrow for sin; still less the practice of penance. It means the total re-orientation of life. When our Lord faced the legalism that marked religion in His time He demanded that people repent, meaning that they should turn away completely from putting their trust in the observance of rites and precepts, and that they should look toward God and begin to think in terms of the mind of God. They were to think like God and not like mere men. Their whole being was to be orientated toward God.

For modern men and women repentance must involve, in a very real sense, the turning to God from immersement in a purely scientific outlook, from the spirit which lives and moves and has its being in a three-dimensioned world and which limits possibility to what can be proved under laboratory conditions. We must repent of limiting God to what can be scientifically demonstrated, and turn our lives towards the great dimension of depth, towards the world of the spiritual which has its own laws and its own forms of verification. And within the Church we must repent of our ecclesiasticism, of reducing religion to forms and practices, confusing the life of the Spirit with a life of ethical decency and conventional behaviour. We must repent, turning our gaze towards horizons vaster than the ecclesiastical order. We must cease to confuse true religion with what we observe it to be within the very cold and conventional confines of church life. We must re-orientate our minds towards God, coming into fresh touch with the realities of the spiritual order which " eye hath not seen, nor ear heard, neither have entered into the heart of man ".

Faith, too, is involved, evangelical faith. True faith in Jesus Christ, faith which saves, the faith which the Holy Spirit creates in the believer, is something much more than assent to propositions about Jesus Christ. The plain truth is that one may assent to the most orthodox ideas about the Incarnation and the Atonement and the Resurrection of the Son of God and remain a pure pagan. Saving faith is faith which, having calmly taken into account all that can be known about Jesus Christ, ends in a commitment to Jesus Christ Himself as the living Lord. It is, therefore, not a mere acceptance of ideas about Him but a commitment to Him, whereby Jesus Christ becomes the Saviour and Lord of one who becomes His servant and follower for ever.

The life of God in the soul of man, the reality of personal religion, is our most decisive need in the world of to-day. The main Christian issue as it confronts us to-day is not the same issue that confronted religion after the First World War. At that time the great task was to set Revelation over against Humanism; the Word of God over against the word of man. That task was admirably undertaken by Karl Barth and by those who approached the problems of our time under the inspiration of a rediscovered doctrine of the Word. We must continue, it is true, to set the everlasting Word of God over against its human rivals. But to-day the main issue is different. As events have developed in these last years, as crusading forces begin to marshal upon the spiritual frontiers of the world, determined to illumine the abyss and to organize the anarchy which separates us from to-morrow, the issue has come to be Christian life over against pagan dynamism. Life must be matched with life; the life of God in the soul created by the Holy Ghost must meet the life created by the demonic powers. The Word of God that is proclaimed over against all relativism, and naturalism, and every philosophy which competes with it for the interpretation of human life and destiny, must become flesh. It must clothe itself in regenerate life through the operation of the Holy Spirit. To-day we need men more than we need ideas, or rather we need ideas that have become flesh.

I know of no more perfect symbol to express what our attitude should be at this time, if we would express our faith in the given Word and manifest the response which that Word merits when it challenges us, than the crest of John Calvin. We usually regard Calvin as an austere thinker, and so he was, the architect of the theological system which alone can match the massive thought structure of Thomas Aquinas. But Calvin was not merely a man of the mind; he was supremely a man of the heart. If he made any really original contribution to theology it was his doctrine of the Holy Spirit. John Calvin's crest is a flaming heart in an open hand, with the interpretative words in Latin, " My heart I give thee, Lord, eagerly and sincerely ". Here in emblematic form is the meaning of a true response to the Word of God, a passionate heart, symbol of undying devotion to Jesus Christ, in a hand, the emblem of unceasing service in the cause of the Lord and Redeemer. What the Holy Spirit does in making the Word effectual in the human soul is what the Church and the world most need to-day, a response to the Word of God with all the passion and devotion of the heart and all the unceasing service of the hand. Thus mind and heart and hand together make themselves servants of the Word, heralds and harbingers of the kingdom of Christ.

3

LET THE CHURCH
LIVE ON THE FRONTIER

THE CHURCH'S PLACE IS THE FRONTIER. ITS destiny is bound up with a frontier life, for that is the life to which God has called it. When the Christian Church belongs too completely to any community or nation, to any civilization or culture, to any generation or era, it ceases to be its true self and fails to fulfil its destiny. When the Church is no longer mobile, when the pioneer spirit has left it, when missionary vision no longer inspires it, when a challenge to high adventure under God fails to awaken a response in prophetic words and redemptive deeds, the Church is dead. It is dead, even should it be acclaimed as the most venerable institution of which a nation, a culture, or an era can boast. For the Church is truly the Church solely in the measure in which it lives a pilgrim life upon the road of God's unfolding purpose, keeping close to the rugged boundaries of His ever-expanding Kingdom.

By the Church we do not mean any single visible society or institution which may make exclusive claim to be called the Church. We mean rather the corporate group of those societies called Churches which profess allegiance to Jesus Christ as their divine Head and regard themselves as members of

His body. We are thinking of the Church visible and militant, which, in virtue of the fact that its boundaries are now co-extensive with the inhabited globe, is entitled to the name " ecumenical ".

By the Frontier, we understand that place where life is lived most closely to man's need and God's purpose. It is the region where issues are clean-cut, where good and evil stand in sharpest contrast, where sunset and sunrise are seen and felt most keenly. In this twilight, revolutionary time, this end of an era in which we live, the Christian Church is called afresh to a frontier life. Only upon the Frontier, ready to trek into the unknown, waiting for the Leader's word at midnight or at noonday, can the Church be saved from the fate of institutions that have staked their all upon a human something that Time has marked for dissolution.

There are to-day several frontiers upon which the Church must gird itself for special action. There is, to begin with, the *political Frontier*. This frontier has in recent years flamed suddenly into action. For generations, and in some instances for centuries, it had been quiescent, so far as the Church was concerned. But now upon the political frontier the destiny of mankind is being so radically affected, and the witness of the Church in society so basically challenged, that political issues have assumed unwonted importance. For that reason the voice of the Church needs to sound, like the ancient voices of Amos and Isaiah, in the high places of the nation. In words plain and forthright, it must be made clear to rulers that neither they nor the State dare usurp the authority that belongs to God alone. Governments are but His servants to achieve earthly justice. Beneath them are the foundations of moral law upon which legislation must be built; around them is God's providential rule which will ultimately thwart political action that runs counter to righteousness; above them is Jesus Christ the sovereign Lord of that Kingdom whose supremacy all the rulers of earth must acknowledge or perish. The Church must also proclaim that in God's world there is no such thing as absolute sovereignty for nations any more than for individuals; that power should no longer express itself in imperialistic lordship, but rather in responsible trusteeship for the good of backward nations; that an international order founded upon the will of all peoples is more enduring than that which rests upon the alliance of a few powerful states.

As regards internal politics, it is the Church's duty to sensitize the conscience of a nation, and of all classes and institutions within the nation, so that no group of citizens shall arrogate to themselves perpetual rights and privileges which they deny to others. The Christian Church, to be true to its nature and mission in a state or community, must work for an orchestral expression of social life. No person must suffer ostracism or any form of disability because of the colour of his skin, or the hard misfortune of his lot, but must be permitted to share to the fullest degree in the common life. It is equally part of the Church's responsibility to secure, through its public witness and the constitutional pressure of its members, that there shall be rectitude in the administration of public affairs. In a great city of the United States the statement was recently made, " The Churches of this city are very strong, but the politics are rotten." If such is the case, the church members in that community should blush for very shame.

There is also the *cultural Frontier*. Historically, the Christian Church has influenced culture in all its expressions, and at all the social levels, more than any other institution. It has created a passion for literacy; it has provided the inspiration that produced a Bach and a Rembrandt. The history of Western philosophy would have been totally different had the great Greeks known Moses and the Prophets. Yet the Church has suffered more in the course of its history from the blandishments of secular culture than from the bludgeonings of political tyrants. It has often succumbed to the temptation to express its own unique truth in terms of some category supplied by a culture which had no place for the transcendent light of Revelation. The gates of Hell have rarely prevailed against the historic Church, but, as Hegel boasted, the gates of Reason have. The Church is in peril, and has abandoned the Frontier, when it so infuses its warmth and inspiration into a purely secular culture as to become that culture's soul. That is what the Nazis wished the Christian Church to do, to sanctify the cosmic role and all the ways of the *Herrenvolk*. Many American politicians and educators would like the Church in the United States to assume, as its chief function, that of sanctifying values and canonizing objectives which are presented as spiritual ultimates, and so as substitutes for the goal of Christian devotion. The Church must as truly live upon the frontier of a democratic culture as upon the frontier of a totalitarian culture.

LET THE CHURCH LIVE ON THE FRONTIER

One of the crucial problems facing the Church at the present time is the fact that modern secular thought has largely been emptied of the great Christian concepts. It has been exceedingly difficult, in consequence, to communicate Christianity and Christian ideas to our contemporaries. There is, however, one great hope; the march of events has shattered the secularistic world-view. Such categories as " self-realization ", " self-expression ", " innate goodness ", " the autonomy of reason ", in which humanistic culture gloried, have been " weighed in the balance and found wanting ". The great prophetic words, " Cease ye from man ", and, " Earth, earth, earth, hear the word of the Lord ", have once again taken on new meaning. The Second World War has created a situation in which the classical terms of the Christian religion have suddenly been filled with fresh and meaningful content. People are now willing to listen to, and are eager to understand, the terms Sin and Suffering, Judgment and Mercy, Freedom and Serfdom, Saviour and Redemption, Sacrifice and Atonement. In the cultural reconstruction which is now under way, and which must be as radical and thorough-going as its political and social counterpart, the central categories of the Christian religion have a major part to play. If the Church does not lose its insight into the faith to which it is heir, it will have a matchless opportunity to interpret the Christian Gospel, and to make the great verities of the Christian faith burningly real for men and women whose proud cultural palace has been blitzed.

It is perfectly apparent, however, that the Church's task in the realm of culture is not going to be easy.

The modern theologian has as difficult a problem as the modern poet. The poet's task in our time is, as Archibald MacLeish points out, to enter into and to describe the experiences of modern men and women which for them are still inarticulate, in such a way that he shall make them see and understand themselves, give them a voice that they may utter things hitherto unutterable, and make vocal their abysmal longings. No modern poet has succeeded more fully in this task than T. S. Eliot. His *Wasteland*, to use the words of MacLeish, " precipitated the cloudy confusion of an age and made human and tragic what had before been impersonal and intellectual and for the most part unseen." In England, two lay writers, Dorothy Sayers and C. S. Lewis, have made the language of Christianity live afresh for their fellow countrymen. On this side of the Atlantic, Reinhold Neibuhr, and more recently F. W. Dillistone in his book, *The Significance of the Cross*, make modern men and women feel that they understand their predicament, that they know their language, that the great classical terms of the Christian religion open up new solutions for their problems and offer healing medicine for their wounds. In such a situation, it is high time to stop bandying around terms which had their source in the theological struggles of yesterday, and which fail now to convey clear meaning.

The time has come to resuscitate and reinterpret the glorious term *Evangelical*, which is so Biblical in its background and so positive in its content. Let the Church, standing upon the Frontier of culture, with the light of a new sunrise streaming upon it, open up the facets of divine splendour that are contained in the Evangel. Let it show how the Gospel is relevant to the manifold ills of the human mind and spirit, for which it alone has the basic answer. We have witnessed no more unholy horseplay in recent American history than the sport of attaching to people labels whose import is only vaguely apprehended. Anyone who has a desire to pillory and damn someone else, whether in religion or politics, has only to call him a " fundamentalist " or a " modernist ", a " conservative " or a " liberal ", a " communist " or a " fascist ", as the case may be, and his malevolent purpose is achieved.

But if there is to be a restoration of true Christian culture, the Church must use all legitimate means to secure that in every centre of education, provision is made for the teaching of the Christian religion. But the Faith must be taught by men and women who understand and believe it, and who present it with as much enthusiasm as that with which the great teachers of science, literature, or art, teach their courses. In the words of the distinguished American already referred to, Archibald MacLeish, the late Librarian of Congress, let us be done with the pseudo-intellectuals who " prefer the safety of a spinsterish and impotent intellectualism to the risk of affirmation and belief." Let us repudiate the teacher of religion who " is afraid to defend his convictions for fear he may defend them in the wrong company ". Let the Church and Christian culture beware of the men who exult in the " antiseptic air of objectivity ", and who " by that sublimation of the mind prepared the mind's disaster ".

There is, finally, the *missionary Frontier*. That is

where the ultimate problems of the Christian Church are to-day. Knowing what it is, sure of its faith, radiating its light, the Christian Church must deal with the supreme question of an adequate missionary approach to the world. Basic to any such approach is Christian unity. This is no time for Christians to retire within their ecclesiastical boundaries and immerse themselves in the contemplation of their denominational glory. It is rather a time when they should move out from the centre to the circumference of their corporate witness. Upon their ecclesiastical boundary let them greet Christians who approach them from the other side of the Frontier. There let them share with one another the truth and experience which God has taught each group in the course of its history. It is a time for Christians of different backgrounds and traditions to listen to one another, to pray with and for one another, to work together in causes of common concern. It is a time for them, with due loyalty to truth, in the name of Christ, and for the sake of men, to give, as far as possible, visible, and even organizational, expression to their unity. Any Christian church to-day which, in the light of the Christian revelation and of history, presumes to be the one and only Church, closing its frontier to Christian unity and immersing its members in the exclusive thought of its own greatness, betrays Jesus Christ and is guilty of blasphemy. Not only so, but every tendency towards " churchism ", which would make the Church an end in itself, is a reproduction in the religious realm of that demonism which has been the bane of modern political life.

The physical unity of the world, and the international character of contemporary problems, make the unity of the Christian Church still more imperative. As regards steps toward unity and eventual union, the natural thing is that those Churches which have native affinities or have stemmed from a common stock and so belong to the same ancestral tradition, should enter, first of all, into organic relations. But in no case should a church union take place for reasons of pure expediency, nor because the attitude toward doctrine and Christian witness has reached so low an ebb in both that there is no reason why they should stand apart; for they are bound together by the common bond of indifference. Church union becomes real and fruitful only when leaders and people enter upon it for positive Christian reasons, and because they can no longer justify their separate existence to themselves or to the world.

But let us beware of any form of church co-operation or union which merely brings into being a more centralized and powerful bureaucracy. The danger which Protestant Christianity faces at the present time in the United States is the over-centralization that obtains in some of the major denominations. The problems of the religious frontier in this land would be more creatively met by a united Christian approach upon a regional basis, than by the establishment of a national bureaucracy which would presume to deal with all the religious problems of the country. If the latter were carried through, there would result an even more lamentable chasm than now exists between church leaders and the common people, between the ecclesiastical bureaucrat and the religious life of the nation. For that reason we believe that the projected merger of a number of religious organizations in this country should be carefully studied in the light of the challenge that comes from the great natural regions of the nation. It should be entered into only if it were positively certain that the specific problems of those areas would be adequately dealt with through the new organization. If that is not done, regional leadership will not be developed, yet such leadership is no less important than national leadership. We need to develop men and women capable of bringing to bear upon the religious problems of a great region the feel of the land, the inspiration of its history and literature, the pathos of its social problems, the heritage and aspirations of its people, as well as an intimate knowledge of the successes and failures of the Christian Church within its borders. Annual ecclesiastical gatherings that deal only with questions of national, ecumenical, or world magnitude, never begin to touch the real questions that affect the progress of Christianity.

But Christian unity in itself is not enough to lead the Church to the missionary Frontier and keep it there. Evangelistic fervour is needed, a passion to make Jesus Christ known, and loved, and obeyed among men. It is high time that the traditional Churches realized that the evangelistic efforts of the so-called sects and cults are much more successful than their own. How pathetic beyond words that any group of Christians should feel that a beautiful and impressive liturgical service can ever become a substitute, in the experience of men and in the sight of God, for evangelistic fervour that reaches the unchurched, and transforms them into new men and women in Christ! One has heard it said, with a feeling of shame and dismay, by representative churchmen, that there are groups in society who cannot be reached, nay, who should not be reached, by their particular denomination. The plain truth is, that any local church or any Christian denomination which is unable to devise a missionary approach to a specific social group in the area where that church or denomination has responsibility, fails in the acid test to which every religious organization must ultimately submit. This applies equally in the homeland and on the foreign field. Let no religious group be unkindly critical of any other which God is manifestly using to lead men to a new life in Christ, even although objectionable features may attend the missionary effort, unless the critics themselves are able to achieve spiritual results of a similar order without those features.

For many, all too many, years, forward movements of one kind or another in the Christian Church, have taken place at the inspiration or under the leadership of extremist elements, to the religious right or left. The hour has arrived for the Centre to move towards the Frontier. Credally speaking, the great Centre in Protestant Christianity has not been disloyal to the historic Christian faith. But it has been confused, cold, and complacent, living at a distance from the frontier realities of life and thought and the purpose of God. It has been passive and inarticulate. It has been like a ship passing through the locks of the Panama Canal that is dragged forward by electric engines to the right and left of it, and steadied in the channel by two others in the rear. But the moment comes when the cables are detached fore and aft, and the great liner, now under its own engine power and the guidance of its own officers, moves out of the narrow channel, past palm-clad islands, into the ocean highway where the shore is soon lost to view.

Enough of the forward tug of political edict, and social pressure, and spiritual aberration; enough of the backward drag of prejudice and convention! Let the Church, as from a "peak in Darien", scan the ocean vastness of its true sphere of action; and upon the power generated by a deepened experience of Jesus Christ and a new sense of its destiny, and with the Captain Himself in charge, head for the Frontier to which God calls it beyond the horizon of its present vision.

4

THE PERIL OF A VACUUM

A SUPREME PERIL THREATENS OUR GENERATION. IT is a spiritual vacuum, the opening of a hollow void in the souls of men. In the lives of multitudes of people an appalling emptiness is forming.

Ours is not, of course, the first generation to be marked by a vacuum. Emptiness was the leading trait in the Israel of Jeremiah's time. The great prophet describes the hollow souls of his countrymen in two classical passages which, when read in modern translations, take on new meaning. " Following after the Bubble, they bubbles became ", is how George Adam Smith translates the familiar words, " They have walked after vanity, and are become vain ". (Jeremiah 2 : 5). Or in the rendering of Moffatt, " They went after empty idols and became empty themselves ". Using another figure, Jeremiah thus describes the spiritual emptiness of his countrymen: " They have forsaken me the reservoir of fresh water and hewn out cisterns for themselves, leaky cisterns, that can hold no water ". (Jer. 2 : 13, Moffatt's rendering.) The rejection of God and the pursuit of substitutes for Him created a vacuum in the soul of Israel.

European history in the twentieth century provides momentous illustrations of such a vacuum. The Europe to which Hitler and Mussolini became heirs was a Europe which had become hollow. Fascism, well described as " doctrineless nihilism ", was merely the last phase in a process of dissolution. In the period between the two wars, life became spiritually empty. Men no longer pursued great ends in common. Moral and political anarchy was rampant. There was no vision, no hope; God was dead to all intents, as Nietzsche had said He was. Suddenly the empty temple of the European soul was filled with new gods, the gods of tradition, blood and soil. In the name of these gods a new order of hate was proclaimed. Then came history's greatest war, which raged six years. During this period millions of people, in both the Axis and satellite nations, fought passionately for their gods and the new order—desperate souls, filled with the illusion of a millenial kingdom.

The horror of a vacuum haunts Europe again. How can light pierce the bottomless abyss of disillusionment which in these last months has opened in the souls of millions? How can love take the place of hate? How can meaning be restored to people who dreamed of an imperial future, a future which they were convinced lay awaiting them in the lap of destiny, and which vanished into air just as their hands were clutching victory?

Even in the Europe delivered from Axis domination, a phase of the vacuum has appeared. Millions who belonged to the underground organizations have ceased to make moral distinctions. It became second-nature for young patriots to employ the most morally repulsive methods to thwart and eliminate their hated foes. A distinguished Frenchman, who was close to the underground movement in his country, has recently

THE PERIL OF A VACUUM

expressed this concern, "How can a moral sense be reborn in youth who have come through this terrible era?"

The same vacuum will undoubtedly appear in Asia after the bubble of the New Order has burst. We are going to look into the eyes of Japanese who, in a sense totally different from that of the "man with the hoe", will have "the emptiness of ages" in their faces—but of ages that never came. The prospect of an abysmal vacuum in a large part of Europe and of Asia, following the close of the recent war, will present one of the gravest spiritual problems in history. What spirit or spirits shall re-occupy the empty, desolate shrines of human devotion? How can re-education take place in a spiritual vacuum? What shall be the immediate future of the Christian religion in both those areas?

The peril of a vacuum is by no means confined, however, to Europe and Asia. It began to appear ominously in Anglo-Saxon civilization after World War I and its menace has grown steadily ever since. At the present moment, as the pace of triumph quickens in the Orient, and the United States and Great Britain look forward to the approach of victory, the prospect of a new void increases.

A disturbing emptiness has been making its presence felt in many spheres of thought and life. Poets have sensed its sinister on-coming. T. S. Eliot wrote in the twenties :

> We are the hollow men,
> We are the stuffed men,
> Leaning together,
> Headpiece filled with straw.

Voices have been singing for years " out of empty cisterns and exhausted wells ". Cultural inspiration has lost its springs. Setting themselves to " grow in the wrong earth ", men found they had no roots. To-day, as another poet-prophet puts it, we hear " voices rising up from the cities where the people are, but only voices ". The meaningful word is absent. People abound whose " strained, time-ridden faces are distracted from distraction by distraction ". The things they are interested in are no more than " vacuities fringed with lace ".

To be more specific, let us review some major fields in our cultural situation. No great unifying idea informs and interprets our culture. No luminous and compelling purpose is offered as the supreme goal of devotion. Philosophy's excessive, almost morbid preoccupation, with the problem of knowledge, has led to Logical Positivism. Logical Positivism denies that such problems as God and the soul are real, and devotes itself to a study of language, with a view to purging an increasing tendency towards emptiness of concept. Nature dissolves in mathematical fictions. As for modern art, through its exclusive concern with expression, it bears all the symptoms of decay. The great Spanish writer, Miguel de Unamuno, once remarked, when introduced to an exhibition of modernistic art in Paris, " This art is so modern that it will never be ancient! " The vacuity of contemporary literature is notorious. It is " filled with fancies and empty of meaning ". The individual is lost in the mass; the writer does not serve a cause; only expression matters. But how could it be otherwise? Modern men of letters have cut themselves off from literature's

THE PERIL OF A VACUUM

chief source of inspiration. For the first time in the history of English letters since Beowulf and Chaucer, we have a generation of writers who are totally ignorant of the Bible. And the quality of their writing reflects the vacuum in their culture.

Equally disturbing is the emptiness in the realm of politics. Our statesmen are so naïvely shallow and short-sighted that in their international planning righteousness is given second place to security. They fail to realize that security is like pleasure. When it is pursued as an end in itself by a man or a nation, or even a world order, it can never be grasped. What Hecate, the goddess of the underworld, said to the witches about the ill-starred Macbeth is everlastingly true: " Security is mortals' chiefest enemy ". To learn righteousness and to do justly is much more important for great powers than the attempt to establish their own security without reference to the moral foundations of the universe. As T. S. Eliot has put it in *Murder in the Cathedral*:

> Those who put their faith in worldly order
> Not controlled by the order of God,
> In confident ignorance, but arrest disorder,
> Make it fast, breed fatal disease,
> Degrade what they exalt.

In the sphere of religion, the peril of a vacuum is no less real. Liturgical pageantry tends more and more to take the place of the great simplicities of worship. A false aestheticism makes many a modern church service an empty show of words and sound and colour. People forget that the content of faith in the God who is worshipped is infinitely more important than the particular form which His worship may take.

The God and Father of our Lord Jesus Christ is no finicky snob or childish faddist. Could anything be more fatuous than the attempt to solve the problem of faith by the symbols of form? Religious reality is what we need, " Spirit with spirit meeting, God and sinner treating ".

Doctrinal definiteness in religion is discouraged in the interests of sentimental goodwill. The historic creeds which, despite their human character, are freighted with divine truth, the sacraments that mediate to the believing soul the reality of God's grace, are decried as divisive, as obstacles to human fellowship. It was recently proclaimed in a gathering of religious thinkers that the kind of Christianity which is needed is what the speaker called " Oceanic Christianity ". This would appear to be a great eclectic abyss, without discernible shore-lines, where all streams mingle and are lost, with no established ports where voyaging begins or ends. The boundless ocean may be an appropriate symbol of eternity and of life beyond the shores of time; but the true symbol of a religion which is relevant to history and expresses God's redemptive purpose in history is not the ocean, but the river. For the river has a definite source, and follows a discernible course. The simple fact that its waters are channelled makes the flowing movement of a stream more significant for the lives of men than the vast expanses of the ocean.

What is the answer to the problem of " hollow men ", to the inward nihilism which imperils our generation, to the vague romanticism which empties the Christian religion of positive content and redemptive power?

THE PERIL OF A VACUUM

The nihilistic void which plagues our time cannot be met by any amount of concentration upon the physical side of the human problem. Everything that can be done in the interests of relief, rehabilitation, and reconstruction in the devastated areas of the world and among people who have suffered indirectly through the war must be carried out with speed and lavish generosity. But no welfare scheme will touch the real problem in any country. Much more than bread and houses and work and physical security will be required. As regards the future of life even in the victorious nations, the following reminder by a distinguished British writer, Herbert Read, is most timely: " There is a danger that all our national planning of society may give us homes fit for heroes but nothing to be heroic about, security from every disease except boredom, plenty in the land but a platitudinous emptiness which spreads like a leprosy over the mind." (In *This Changing World*, edited by J. R. M. Brumwell, p. 264.)

The external organization of life is equally inadequate to solve the prevailing emptiness in souls and institutions. We can begin to deal with the real problem of our time only when empty, darkened human spirits are turned to the light. Not organization, but orientation towards the central Truth and meaning of existence, a new direction for thought and striving, a new vision and a new hope, is needed. It is here that Christian theology can help. The great doctrines of the Faith serve like telescopic lenses to make the ultimate meaning of existence plain and real to the soul that is willing to look through them.

But an apprehension of the truth about life is not

enough. Something must happen to life itself, for to know about life is not to live it. To know about God is not to know Him. The Word that illumines the soul must become flesh within the soul. Orientation must be followed by renewal. Theology reaches its frontier when it brings the human spirit face to face with the living reality of God as the source of light and life and when it makes plain that the next step is not thinking but deciding, not belief but faith, not intellectual patronage but spiritual surrender.

God's coming into life is the only adequate answer to the problem of spiritual emptiness. With His entry, life is renewed from within. The soul is cleansed, new wells of refreshment are opened, love assumes control, responsible selfhood with a passion for righteousness is developed. The desolate void becomes a source of loveliness and a centre of power.

But under what conditions does this happen? By what definite attitude of the soul does God and all the "charismatic profundities of life" (Franz Werfel) enter into the place of emptiness? The clue is found in the experience of a representative and symbolic figure. Pascal, one of the supreme intellects of all time, came to the point where the resources of reason failed him. The God-Idea of the "philosophers and scholars" could not fill his inner void. He longed for a Presence. In a moment of spiritual illumination, in a rapture of total surrender, he affirmed his faith, and gave his life to another: "God of Jesus Christ. My God and thy God. Thy God shall be my God." The man of science became a saint; he belonged thereafter to a new order of life, the order of Charity.

Sainthood, a twentieth century expression of

Christian sainthood, is what our generation needs. The only people who can meet the present crisis are men and women who have seen life's meaning and experienced its reality in Jesus Christ. What our generation with its haunting vacuum needs more than anything else is to learn how men become sons of God by inward renewal. The Gospel which speaks of God's gracious approach to men in Christ, which brings into their lives light, love, and hope, and gives them something to live for and a meaningful place within God's great scheme of things, is now, as it always has been, the answer to meaningless lives.

" Oh for more of God in my soul! Oh this pleasing pain! " exclaimed David Brainerd, an eighteenth century saint. God in the soul is life's supreme pleasure, for in the divine communion every human longing is met. God in the soul is also life's most exquisite pain, for the soul in whom God dwells becomes a sharer in His love passion for men. The love of God is both rapture and suffering. This rapture and this suffering are the ultimate antidote to " hollow men ", and the one answer to contemporary nihilism.

5

THE CRUCIAL ALTERNATIVES

THE INTELLECTUAL CLIMATE OF OUR TIME IS NOT particularly noted for the number of convictions it produces. One conviction, however, is all pervasive among thoughtful students of human affairs. It is the conviction that history has reached a watershed, one of the great divides in the fortunes of mankind.

There are, of course, differences of opinion as to where precisely this watershed is located. For some it is located within our civilization. Western civilization, they say, has entered upon its " time of troubles " but it will succeed in making the adjustment that is necessary for its continuance. For others the watershed is located at the end of our civilization. According to this view, to-day is bounded by a dark, unknown to-morrow. Another civilization, history's twenty-second, will take shape in due course; but in the immediate future life's main stream will plunge into a deep gorge on the shadow side of progress, becoming lost for a period in sunless night. For a third group the watershed is located at the end of all history. The inevitable misuse of atomic energy, so the members of this group believe, will cause collective suicide on this planet and human history will come to a close.

Without committing ourselves to any one of these

positions, one thing is clear from both history and revelation. Each time that mankind faces a major crisis, its one hope lies in adjusting itself to the Eternal Order, that is, to the laws and purposes of God to which men must conform if they are to prosper in God's world. While it is not the function of the Christian Church to save a civilization, Christians must be made aware that very crucial alternatives confront the Church and the world at the present time. Three alternatives are particularly crucial.

THE GLORY OF GOD OR THE DISHONOUR OF MAN

The first alternative is this: *The Church must live for the glory of God or the world will mourn the dishonour of man.* There is a familiar question about the life of man which runs, " What is the chief end of man? " It is the first question of a religious nature with which some of us were ever confronted. The answer is incomparable for its truth and beauty: " Man's chief end is to glorify God, and to enjoy Him forever." The " glory " of God, in Biblical language, means the unveiled splendour of His nature, in particular, the splendour of His goodness, the majesty and might that pledge the fulfilment of His redemptive concern. To glorify God is to make Him visible, to make manifest the splendour of His loving-kindness, the majestic instancy of His passion for men. Man's highest excellency, the only way whereby he can fulfil his destiny and be truly man, is to live for the glory of God. To do so men must live in such a way that God's inmost nature and His deepest purpose for human life may appear in their individual lives and corporate relations.

To live for the glory of God in this Biblical sense is something much more personal and significant than to portray the Divine splendour in monuments of stone, in pictures of ravishing appeal, in music that enraptures the heart. There is no aesthetic substitute for the splendour of God in human life and relations. So, too, no masterpiece of literature, no system of sound doctrine, however impressively it may interpret God and the ways of God, can be a substitute for the glory of holy living, for the manifestation of divine love in action, in a word, for life which is instrumental in making God visible. God is never glorified when He is a mere object of human admiration, however ecstatic and sincere that admiration may be; He is glorified only when He becomes the subject of human living, the Lord of man's pilgrim way.

One or two illustrations will make our meaning plain. " I beseech thee, show me thy glory ", Moses prayed (Exod. 33 : 18). He had been charged with the leadership of a people to whom God had given His law. Now as a spiritual adventurer, before ordering Israel to strike its tents and march for the Land of Promise, he craved a manifestation of Deity which would strengthen his faith that God was with His people on the wilderness trail. What he sought was not an overwhelming, miraculous evidence of God's existence, but rather a proof that God was on the road with Israel and that Israel was in the ways of God. Centuries later an exiled seer, Ezekiel, saw the glory of God burst like a sunrise over the mountains of Moab. Flashing across the Dead Sea and up the Judean wilderness, it entered the temple through its eastern portals. But the presence of God in the temple was not designed to give splendour to a shrine, but to create a well-spring in the desert. Mysterious alchemy! God's glory in the sanctuary gave birth to a river. This river, flowing out through the same portals where the Glory came in, made the wilderness blossom at its passing. Coming at length to the Dead Sea, the waters changed nature's vastest sepulchre into a place of teeming life (Ezek. 43 : 1–4; 47 : 1–12).

In " the fullness of time " the splendour of God became manifest in a Person. Of Jesus Christ it was said by those who understood His significance, " We beheld his glory, the glory as of the only begotten of the Father, full of grace and truth " (John 1 : 14). In the life of Christ the splendour of goodness, the majestic movements of God's redemptive love, culminated in a cross which, according to the Fourth Gospel, was the supreme revelation of the divine glory. With unerring insight into the meaning of that cross and the witness of a life that had been renewed by its power, Saint Paul exclaimed in a rapture, " God forbid that I should glory, save in the cross of our Lord Jesus Christ " (Gal. 6 : 14). The apostle reckoned that he could worthily fulfil his destiny only if he entered into the fellowship of suffering that constituted Christ's glory, making himself, in soul and in body, in life and in death, the organ of the unveiled splendour of God. In his Letter to the Ephesians, where doctrine breaks into music, Paul proclaims that it is part of the cosmic mission of the Church to become a textbook for spirits higher than human spirits wherein they may gain insight into the " many coloured wisdom " of God (Eph. 3 : 10).

The meaning of this for the Church and Christians in our day is obvious. No sacramental function can exhaust the Church's role. It must be more than the place where the Word is preached and the Sacraments administered. It must be more than a sociological agent for the welfare of society. It is the Church's supreme function to be the instrument of God's glory in every phase of life, individual and collective.

Either the Church is willing to serve God thus; either Christians "copy God" as Paul said they should, and become "perfect as your father in heaven is perfect", as Jesus said they must, or a crucial alternative will become manifest. Men will live in dishonour, without lustre or splendour, because they will be living "without God in the world". A man who lives for his own glory, to make manifest his own egotism and to proclaim that he is a god in his own right, will in the end cease to be man. He will become an empty shadow, a wizened corpse, a sepulchral ghost of his true self. The same fate will overtake the institutions of society if they attempt to be ends in themselves.

And it is just this that has happened. In a marvellous sentence Jeremiah describes the tragic process of dehumanization which overtook the men of his day. In our King James version the words run: "They have walked after vanity, and are become vain" (Jer. 2:5). James Moffatt renders the passage, "They went after empty idols and became empty themselves." And George Adam Smith, with his glowing Celtic imagination and a fine sensitivity to Hebrew shades of meaning, translates the thought of the prophet: "Following after the Bubble they bubbles became."

That is a matchless description of millions of our contemporaries. They and their objectives have become empty bubbles. The presence of a dread vacuum in every area of modern life is a witness to the tragic fact that our generation has made the wrong choice. We sought the glory of man and we witness man's dishonour. We must seek the glory of God, if we would achieve his renewal.

The Frontier with Christ or the Sanctuary without Him

The second alternative might be formulated thus: *The Church must stand with Christ on the frontiers of the world, or it will lose him in the sanctuaries at home.* Jesus Christ is the Lord, the "pioneer and perfecter" of the faith that proclaims that the future lies with God and his purpose. As the personal head of the Church and the chief agent of God's redemptive purpose, Christ's supreme concern and place of action is the Frontier. He dwells where the danger is greatest, where the struggle is fiercest, where the need of advance is most crucial, where new areas of life must be won for His kingdom. There He awaits venturesome spirits to rally to His banner. He has not handed over His terrestrial interests to any proxy as hierarchical Christianity believes He has. He lives where life's problems are acutest, not in the abodes of complacency or where substitutes have usurped His authority.

The Christian Church, if it would enjoy Christ's personal leadership, must once again go to Him "without the camp", beyond the orbit of so much that is done and thought in His name. The Church, to be truly the Church, must never cease to move towards the frontiers of life, responsive to the words of the Supreme Commander, mobile to meet new situations as they arise. Happily, the Church of to-day stands, as never before in history, on the geographical frontiers of the world. Keeping vigil at the outmost bounds of human habitation, it must fulfil its destiny as a world missionary community.

There are several crucial frontiers in our time where Christ stands and where the Church must stand with him in faith and obedience. If it does, these frontiers will flame with the splendour of God and resound to the tread of His ongoing purpose. There is, to begin with, the frontier of physical need. The Christian Church to-day is summoned by Christ to minister to human need in every place on earth where need is found. To be worthy of the tradition that goes back to the hills and highways of Galilee, the Church must care for human suffering. There is hunger and famine in our world; there are uprooted lives and shattered homes; there are diseased and derelict bodies in greater numbers than ever before in history. Christ is concerned to show compassion. The Christian Church must stand with her Lord, and in a practical way manifest His compassion on this frontier of suffering and dereliction. Woe betide the Church, or any group within the Church, if credence is given to the idea that merely by preaching or by the mere prophetic announcement of truth, God is fully glorified and the Church's role fulfilled. No; visible and tangible expression must be given to what the New Testament writer meant when he said about

Christ, " He had compassion on the multitude ", and what Christ Himself meant when He said, " Give ye them to eat ". Wherever or whenever the Christian Church comes to believe that it can fully witness to its Lord by words alone, or by anything which can be fulfilled simply by speaking or writing, then the Church is apostate and has ceased to be the Church of Jesus Christ.

Yet a frontier does exist which is concerned with speaking. There is an evangelistic frontier where the Church must stand with Christ and proclaim with fresh meaning: " Behold the Lamb of God that taketh away the sin of the world." To-day the frontier of Evangelism is on the edge of an unparalleled void. There is an abyss of spiritual emptiness, an awesome chasm which, like a vast medieval moat, engirdles the life of humanity at the present time. No forward movement can take place until this terrible abyss is illumined and bridged. Within this void are religions and philosophies, nations and institutions, laws and customs, in full process of disintegration. For the Church to stand with Christ upon this frontier means to flash the light of His Gospel into the void, to interpret to men their predicament, to concentrate their gaze upon a Face that merits their loyalty, to summon them to become His disciples. Christian evangelism, using as its instrument the Gospel and the great concepts of the Christian faith, has to-day an unprecedented missionary opportunity. In a disintegrating secular order let it rally broken, yearning, despairing people to a new centre of meaning and a new source of strength.

If the representatives of evangelical Christianity refuse to stand on the frontier of this void, its rivals, who are already there and eagerly at work, will bring their own new order out of the chaos of our time. The strains of the Communist " International ", vibrant with passion, give new hope to millions who acclaim the red banner. Listen:

> Arise, ye prisoners of starvation! Arise, ye wretched of the earth! For justice thunders condemnation, a better world's in birth. No more tradition's chain shall bind you. Arise, ye slaves! No more in thrall. The world shall rise on new foundations. You have been naught: you shall be all. . . .

With hearts compassionate as well as passionate and a purer sense of justice, Christians must outclass Communists in the relevancy of their approach to the total human situation. When Communism, proclaiming, " You have been naught: you shall be all ", sets a man-God, an oligarchically controlled proletariat in the place of God, as the supreme object of devotion, Christians must proclaim the glory of the God-man, the Man of Sorrows, who is the true Saviour and Lord of life. A renascent Romanism stands also as a rival on the frontier of the abyss. Resurgent clericalism, proclaiming a Church-God, summons men to its allegiance. The hour has struck for Protestant Christianity to affirm afresh the sole Lordship of Jesus Christ over all life and His sovereign right to determine the bounds of His Church and the identity of those who belong to it. It is a time for the closest co-operation and understanding between evangelical Christians. What is at stake is the organization under God of human life in the Church and society. With robust faith and decision the Church must equally reject the humanitarianism which elevates distressed people into the throne of Deity, and the clericalism which sets the Church in the place of the Almighty.

But should the Protestant Church fail to stand with Christ on the frontier of the contemporary void, what will the alternative be? The secular order will be organized by Communism and the religious order by Romanism. And at the home seat of Protestant Christianity the Presence will leave the sanctuaries. No glorification of God in terms of architectural grandeur, gorgeous liturgy, social prestige, political power, can secure Christ's presence in the Church. If church men and church women refuse to stand by Christ on the frontier of an old order that is dying and another that agonizes in birth, then the Protestant Church, both at the congregational level and at the level of a World Council, will become, through lack of loyalty to the Christ of the Frontier, a monument to the memory of God instead of a monument to His glory.

Apocalyptic Hope or Contemporary Despair

There is, however, a third crucial alternative: *The Church must keep alive the apocalyptic hope or succumb to contemporary despair.* A freezing pessimism begins to benumb not a few leaders of our generation in Church and State and in society at large. The most concerned men of our time are the atomic scientists who have constituted the Emergency Committee to inform the public of the dangerous possibilities that confront the world. In Christian circles disillusionment has become so complete and faith has grown so faint that the exultant note is absent from Church councils and assemblies. Some have become Christian Stoics who, facing the possibility that history may come to an end, believe that the most we may expect from now onwards is the development of Christian personality within history and the hope of immortality beyond history. Others believe that, in view of the momentous stakes for which statesmen play to-day in the higher spheres of diplomacy, Christian effort should be supremely directed towards influencing political action.

What has happened is plain. The high view of man which inspired thought and action in the Liberal era has been succeeded by a low view of man. Contemporary realism, whether secular or religious, no longer believes in man. But tragically enough, in Christian circles to-day a low view of man is not matched by a high view of God. The Church's supreme need is an adequate view of God, a Christian, Biblical view of the God and Father of our Lord Jesus Christ. We must recover a spiritual vision and an experimental knowledge of Him, to whom the early Christians in the decadent order of the old Roman Empire ascribed blessedness, with rapturous adoration and exultant faith. God is still God. The Lord God omnipotent reigneth; he controls the contingencies of history. What happens to-morrow, the future of civilization, the fate of life upon this planet will ultimately be determined not by scientific wisdom or by political folly, but by God. His glory will break upon the world in fresh splendour. We may have to pass through very hell but there will be a new dawn in history and the Church will be present at the sunrise.

It is a time to explore the apocalyptic hope which is enshrined in the Biblical revelation and is implicit in the great doctrines of the Christian faith. The phantasies of a false apocalypticism, the aberrations of an un-Christian dispensationalism, the theoretical possibilities of scientific wisdom and the practical possibilities of political folly, should not destroy within Christians the Biblical hope that there will be within history a manifestation of God's glory worthy of Christ and the Gospel. "In the land of the living", and not merely in the life everlasting beyond "death's dark vale", history shall witness a worthy consummation of the purpose of God in Christ Jesus our Lord. At the heart of apocalypticism there is a sure and valid hope. The Almighty has a stake in human nature and still more in Jesus Christ. The God and Father of our Lord Jesus Christ has instilled a meaning into the Incarnation, the Atonement, the Resurrection of His Son which will insure that the hopes of prophetic seers and apostolic ambassadors shall be worthily fulfilled. No labour will be vain in the Lord even so far as terrestrial history is concerned. The kingdoms of this world shall become the kingdoms of our God and of His Christ. "Jesus shall reign where'er the sun does his successive journeys run."

Let us therefore greet to-morrow with a cheer. Calmly facing the realities of the contemporary situation, refusing to identify the best in man's world with the reality of God's kingdom, let us brace ourselves to descend, if need be, into the valley of the shadow in the years immediately ahead. But whatever happens, let us at all times and in every circumstance keep alive the faith that Jesus Christ shall one day be acclaimed Lord of all.

With the passage of the years and amid the grimness of the times, the strains of the Scottish metrical version of a great Messianic Psalm become ever dearer and more real.

> His name for ever shall endure;
>   last like the sun it shall:
> Men shall be bless'd in him, and bless'd
>   all nations shall him call.
>
>   . . . . .
>
> And blessed be his glorious name
>   to all eternity:
> The whole earth let his glory fill.
>   Amen, so let it be.

We stake our life upon, we guide our thinking by, we shape our policy in accordance with, the conviction that the risen Christ and a reborn Church shall triumph in history

6

FIRE OR FIRE

THE PERENNIAL HUMAN ISSUE, WHICH IS PARticularly acute and inescapable in our time, has been strikingly expressed by the most distinguished contemporary figure in English verse:

> The only hope, or else despair
> Lies in the choice of pyre or pyre—
> To be redeemed from fire by fire.
>
> . . . . .
>
> We only live, only suspire
> Consumed by either fire or fire.
>
> (T. S. Eliot, *Four Quartets*, " Little Gidding ")

The poet sees clearly and prophetically that our chief problem lies in the realm of passion. Now where passion is the issue, both rational explanation and ethical exhortation are equally impotent to solve it. As Spinoza saw clearly long ago, passion must be met with passion. Only a higher passion can quench a lower. Only the expulsive power of a pure affection can exorcize a sordid lust. In the political realm, where people lack the physical necessities of life, bread and a beneficent Marshall plan can assuage and postpone the explosive vehemence of passion, but they cannot deal basically with the fierce emotions which rend the human heart. Man must be redeemed from fire by fire.

CHRISTIANITY ON THE FRONTIER

Along the whole human front, Fire or Fire is the issue. In its full Christian setting and significance, this means the Fire engendered by man's consuming passion for self-centred satisfaction at all the diverse human levels from the lower to the higher, or the Fire engendered by the Holy Spirit which purifies and inflames man's heart to seek God's kingdom and righteousness. "For the desires of the flesh [unredeemed human nature] are against the Spirit, and the desires of the Spirit are against the flesh; for these are opposed to each other" (Galatians 5: 17, Revised Standard Version).

It thus comes about that the characteristic frontier of life to-day is a thin line between rival forces. Almost gone from the life of mankind is the old geographical frontier which challenged the pioneer settler or explorer. That frontier was a threshold beyond which lay vast territories both new and free. Rapidly passing also is the cultural frontier which stretched as a neutral, changing zone between an advanced and a primitive civilization. Ours is an embattled frontier where passions flame. It is not the frontier between Democracy and Communism. It is a frontier which crosses every other frontier in our time, a blazing frontier where the fire of the "flesh", that is, a consuming passion for the purely human and temporal, meets the fire of the "Spirit" —an equally consuming passion for the divine and eternal.

I

In our discussion of this issue let one thing be quite clear. It is natural for human nature to be passionate. Enthusiasm for something or other is the badge of every true life. " No heart is pure that is not passionate; no virtue is safe that is not enthusiastic." " Purity of heart ", said Kierkegaard, " is to will one thing "; to be devoted with all the ardour of one's being to something that is regarded as of supreme worth. This is heart purity in the formal or psychological sense—a burning sincerity in pursuing what is conceived as the ideal good. The eventual quality of this " purity " as well as the quality of that which its ardour achieves, will depend, of course, upon the particular thing that is willed. Blazing sincerity is not enough. The point is, however, that the insincere or double-minded person, and the person who cherishes no great passion in his life, are sub-human individuals. Only when a man is ardently living for something is he truly human. In this respect a Fascist or a Communist, through his vehement devotion to a cause, is more truly human than a smug and selfish churchman who never becomes excited about anything outside the orbit of his self-interest.

A further observation might be added. The human situation always has in it an element of deep tragedy. To be truly human means more than to show natural enthusiasm: it means an enthusiasm that is concerned in some degree with the state of mankind. Any attitude which limits itself to a cold analysis of the condition of men, or maintains itself in truant aloofness from the problems of human beings, is not merely sub-human; it is anti-human. In this respect many intellectuals, from the Roman Stoics to those thinkers and writers of recent times who, in a tragic era, have lived totally detached from the grim problems of their time, superciliously balconized in their ivory towers, disdaining to show concern and rejecting all commitment, have no real claim to be called " men " in the deep rich meaning of the term. They have been betrayers of truth and of mankind; at most they have had knowledge but not wisdom. They find their prototypes in the sacred books of Hinduism and not in the Christian tradition. How apposite and modern is the following citation made by Toynbee from the Bhagavadgita. " The man whose every motion is void of love and purpose, whose works are burned away with the fire of knowledge, the enlightened call ' learned '. The learned grieve not for those whose lives are fled nor for those whose lives are not fled ". What a devastating picture of many academic types in modern culture the " clercs " of Julien Benda, who have betrayed truth and their time.

In the ultimate sense all truth is personal truth; it has to do with persons and the relations of persons. With all the great defects and tragic consequences of his system, Nietzsche was right in affirming that when a great truth breaks upon the mind it does so as " joyful wisdom ". So too was Unamuno right when he claimed that men should be prepared to be " mad " but not " stupid " (*locos pero no tontos*) inasmuch as everything great in life is done as a *Quijotada*, that is, in the form of devotion to a great idea or cause, which may involve, at the first, ridicule and even persecution at the hands of one's fellows.

II

But the main question remains. To be passionate is not enough. Admitting that the presence of passion is inherent in all true human living, passion can be demonic or divine. It can be a flame " set on fire of hell " or a flame lit at the altar of heaven. It can be a fire fanned by the Devil or a fire kindled and fanned by the Spirit of God.

There is a false demonic fire. Lust that consumes the soul in erotic passion is a fire that keeps great sections of our society in constant conflagration. It inflames in individuals and groups a spirit of orgiastic abandon which reduces to ashes the fairest that life has to offer. It makes charred wreckage of the great sanctities and burns the charter of human trust.

But passion kindled by the lower fire may take on a myriad other forms. Some of these forms are easily recognized as sinister; others have impressive features which win popular esteem. Toynbee has pointed out in his great work, *A Study of History,* that in a disintegrating civilization the trend towards an out-and-out antinomianism is a characteristic feature. The over-arching majesty of a universal law of human behaviour is rejected, and men moved by impulse do what is right in their own eyes. In our time the whims of individuals exulting in their freedom, and the alleged rights of states exulting in their sovereignty, constitute a very great part of the human problem.

Fanaticism which only feels and refuses to think; the passion for martyrdom, not for the vindication of great principles or the advancement of a great cause, but in response to a morbid craving for death, are also expressions of false fire. And yet how moving the spectacle of the sainted Teresa of Avila setting out from home when a little girl in the company of her brother to seek death at the hands of the Moors; and the case referred to by Toynbee of Ignatius of Antioch who, regarding himself as the "wheat of God", longed to be "ground by the teeth of wild beasts into the pure bread of Christ"! "Though I give my body to be burned", said Paul, "and have not charity it profiteth me nothing". Incandescent devotion to a cause, a delirious passion for sacrifice, may be no more than the "offering of false fire before the Lord".

The supreme expression, however, of false fire offered in life's "high places", the one which has the greatest air of sublimity and wins most plaudits, is the passion for glory. A passion for glory may inspire an individual, a class, a race, an institution, even a church, to become god-like in splendour and self-sufficiency, a virtual object of worship, refusing to fulfil God's beneficent purposes. The fires that stir this demonic pursuit of glory on the part of the creaturely and finite are the fires whose flames are fiercest on the frontier of life to-day. It is the age-long aspiration of man to become divine in his own right.

There is no more tremendous symbol of this perenially present and contemporaneously tragic urge in human nature than the arrogant heraldic crest of an Argentine University—the University of Cordoba. A condor, the mighty bird of the Andes, is depicted with wings outspread for a soaring flight, and the legend written in Latin, "*Ut portet nomen meum coram gentibus*" ("That it may carry my fame into the presence of the nations"). Culture, not for the sake of truth, the welfare of man, or the glory of God, but for self-glory! A condor, its wings flame-coloured from the fires of pride, haunts the human side of the thin frontier where fire meets fire.

III

But stronger and purer is the fire that burns on the other side, the God-ward side of the frontier. Faith, where it is genuine Christian faith, is a passion. It is no cold conventional acceptance of inherited beliefs; it is no tepid goodwill towards God and man. It is a passionate commitment of life to a Person, to Jesus Christ, in whom the living, redeeming God meets one in a supreme encounter. Christian faith is to fall in love with Christ, to give one's self in joyous abandon to him as one's Saviour from sin and the Lord of one's life. The soul says to Christ, "My heart I give thee, Lord". What a rapture this commitment can engender! What a deathless passion of devotion it can kindle! In the galleries of history, down all the corridors of time, there are no figures that can match for crusading valour and compassionate tenderness the men and women whom the love of Christ enthralled, who were what they were, who did what they did, because His love constrained them. In a bleak, pessimistic, disintegrating civilization, they shouted in exultation, "Blessed be the God and Father of our Lord Jesus Christ who has blessed us. . . ." In hardship and suffering they became more than conquerors through Him who loved them.

Their highest ambition was to share the fellowship of Christ's sufferings for the sake of His Church. They loved people " in the bowels ", that is, with the affection of Jesus Christ.

Whence this passion? This pure and flaming evangelical passion, which has marked the followers of Christ when they were worthy of their Master and bore witness to the true nature of Christian faith, is a life attitude which the object of faith inspires. " God is a consuming fire ". His holy love burns with a fierce flame all that is unholy. " When I think of God ", Kierkegaard once remarked, " I think of Him upon His throne of sorrow ". For the God who is the object of Christian faith, who gave His Son to be the Saviour of the world, is no truant spectator of the earthly scene, no architype of stoical detachment, no pitiless paragon of aloof Hindu wisdom. Being Himself love, His love wove around human nature when He made it,

> The intolerable shirt of flame
> Which human power cannot remove.

Only when man loves with a pure consuming passion is he really man and at the same time like his Maker.

How significant it is that Jesus Christ who perfectly incarnated God's love and passion bequeathed to His disciples the Holy Spirit as a spirit of flame. " Tongues of fire " became the gift of the risen Christ at Pentecost. His truth burned within His Apostles so that they could not be silent about what they had " seen and heard ". And when they spoke, it was with flaming unction, passionate intensity: " Apostolic madness ", it has been called. The antidote, moreover, which the Apostles prescribed to combat the assault of evil passions " that war against the soul " was to be " filled with the Spirit ". Spirit-filled Christians were regarded in Apostolic times as the only normal and sane Christians. Now as then, nothing but the fire of the Spirit can quench the flames of sordid passion: only the fire of the Spirit can expel the spirit of pride that, in our time, more widely than in any other time, would assume the role of Deity.

IV

It has become fashionable, alas, in many Church circles, especially in the great traditional Churches, to look with profound suspicion upon every manifestation of emotion in religion. The naturalness of emotion in all other realms of human experience is admitted, and its expression in appropriate circumstances is expected and even promoted. But, in religion, emotion is regarded as a perilous intrusion into the conventional proprieties of Church order; a great enthusiasm is frowned upon as a disturbing thing. There has been developed a cult of frigid restraint; liturgical procedures are being promoted whose aesthetic perfection sanctifies spiritual death. As if there was nothing in the Christian religion for people to get really excited about!

When Charles Simeon was carrying on his great ministry in Cambridge University making an impact upon college youth such as has never been surpassed in any centre of learning, a new bell was cast for the belfry tower of a neighbouring church which had this inscription upon it, " Glory to the Church and damnation to enthusiasm!" This sentiment is still expressive of many church communities. They demand that everything religious shall be kept at all times within the bounds and proprieties sanctioned by moderation and good taste. In such circles people " enjoy " religion and their enjoyment is all the more exquisite when they can feel that, in supporting the Church, they are in a subtle way Christ's patrons and not His servants. In the meantime they hurl " damnation " at " Pentecostals " and such-like " fanatics ", and even at those who take a " New Life Movement " too seriously. They forget that there is more hope for uncouth life than for aesthetic death.

It is an impressive fact that in these last years while the traditional forces of religion and democracy are coldly unimpassioned, distinguished representatives of secular culture have been reminding us that the characteristic forces of our time are passionate. This constitutes a very grave peril. Our fear of passion may spell the doom of many things that we dearly cherish. That attitude of mind is deadly which, in Toynbee's fine expression, " sterilizes fanaticism at the cost of extinguishing faith ".

Yet harbingers of promise are not lacking. There are stirrings of faith within the Christian Church. As we approach the time, when after long centuries of division, many Churches will symbolize their oneness in Christ, and form together a " World Council of Churches ", let us remember this. The Holy Spirit who created the Christian Church at the beginning and who inspires every true effort to achieve unity, is a Spirit of flame. May His " tongues of fire " and the passionate ardour His Presence kindles, deliver the

FIRE OR FIRE

Churches from making unity an end in itself, the supreme goal of their aspiring. Rather may the fire of the Spirit transfigure the Churches of the world, making their new-found unity an instrument of the Saviour's deathless passion. Thus fire will be matched with fire upon the flaming frontier of our time, and by fire shall men be redeemed from fire.

7

THE CONTRIBUTION OF THE REFORMED CHURCHES TO CHRISTIAN DOCTRINE

HISTORICALLY SPEAKING, THE REFORMED CHURCHES have given to Christian theology one of its two most monumental and influential treatises. This was done in Calvin's *Institutes of the Christian Religion*. This book which, judged by massiveness and influence, is the greatest single theological work in the history of Protestant thought, has but one peer in the annals of Christian doctrine as a whole, the famous *Summa Theologica* of Thomas Aquinas. Besides being the outstanding theological work produced by Protestant Christianity, it contains the outline and breathes the genius of the Reformed faith. This monument of Christian doctrine, no single element in which can be regarded as entirely original, is, at the same time, the symbol of the fact that Reformed theology is catholic in character. Here we discover in organic cohesiveness and architectonic form the substance of the historic Christian faith. Here a master mind, who was the peer of Erasmus in humanistic studies, set down his theological reflections. These he founded upon Holy Scripture, but not before he had reviewed Christian thought in the patristic, the medieval, and the reformation periods. The essential catholicity of

Reformed theology appears in the circumstance that Calvin's *Institutes* is little more than an extended commentary on the Apostles' Creed. This superbly structural, gloriously catholic treatise of theology constitutes the most outstanding contribution of Reformed Christianity to the history of Christian doctrine.

When we review the history of the Reformed Churches from the time of Calvin to the present day, it becomes clear that their specific contribution to Christian doctrine has been marked by the following characteristics:

One: The Reformed Churches have borne perpetual witness to the importance of doctrine in the life and thought of the Church. They have taken seriously the Biblical precept that God should be loved with the *mind*. The members of these Churches have demanded a reasoned and systematic account of the Christian faith for the satisfaction of their intellectual needs, and as an instrument for practical endeavour. The Reformed Churches, therefore, are by their nature and genius confessional Churches.

Two: Truth, in all its cosmic implications, has been the supreme concern of Reformed theology. It has held that the supreme truth which can engage the mind of man is that of the eternal purpose of God which became unveiled in Jesus Christ, and which has been and continues to be the chief determining factor in human history. This Reformed concern with truth has been supremely directed towards understanding the character and redemptive purpose of God with respect to man and the implications for human conduct, individually and corporately, of the Community of the Elect.

Three: Reformed doctrine when true to its nature begins and ends with God. Here doctrine is not a theology of the Church as in Roman Catholic thought. It is not a theology of the redeemed man, as in Lutheran thought. True to the essential meaning of "theology", Reformed theology is a doctrine of God, begun and pursued in the light of God. The sovereign God, whose redemptive purpose constitutes the scarlet thread of Holy Scripture, whose Son is the Saviour and Lord of life, and whose Church is the true bearer of history, is the theme of Reformed theology, in the same way that the concept of His sovereignty is its organizing principle.

The conception of the sovereignty of God is, of course, not unique in Reformed theology. What is unique is that divine sovereignty is here made the centre and organizing principle of theology. Over against God in His providential rule and redemptive sovereignty, stands man in sinful revolt with his Promethean will and the human misery to which it led.

In this framework are set God's irresistible grace, the Church as the instrument of God's glory, and the state as His vicegerent to achieve order and justice in a sinful world. But in Church and society the ultimate and most significant unit is the "new man" who has been the subject of a saving change effected by the Holy Spirit. Thus the new life in Christ is an ontological reality, and not simply a relationship to God which is maintained by faith. There is a sense in which Calvin, the father of Reformed theology, is more than anything else the theologian of the Holy Spirit, as Augustine is the theologian of grace, Anselm the theologian of the Atonement, and Luther the theologian of justification.

Four: While in Reformed theology of the classical type nature, history, and the soul of man all provide glimmers of the truth about God, it is through revelation as found in Holy Scripture that God becomes known. In the record of God's redemptive dealings with mankind, especially in Jesus Christ, the Word becomes flesh, and in the operation of the Holy Spirit in the human heart and through the Church, the hidden God becomes fully known.

In Reformed theology, worthily so called, the Bible is taken seriously in both its divine and human aspects. Legitimate criticism is encouraged; authenticated truth, whether historical or literary, is made tributary to our understanding of the divine redemptive truth. It cannot be insisted upon too much that the category of revelation is the central category of Reformed theology. The question concerning *what* God has said has primacy over the question as to *how* He said it. While there have been differences among classical Reformed theologians with regard to the meaning of inspiration, it has not affected in any respect their understanding of the primacy and infallible character of the divine revelation in Holy Scripture.

It is important, however to bear in mind that for Reformed theology the truth of divine revelation cannot be established by rational argumentation. The Bible cannot be proved to be the Word of God by any reasoning process. It is known to be the Word of God by Christian believers through the testimony of the Holy Spirit in their hearts. Their own experience of redemption, of which the Spirit is the author, bears witness to the character of God and to the majesty of truth as set forth in Holy Scripture. Had this fact been duly observed the Reformed Churches would have been spared much bitter controversy over the Bible and much futile apologetical effort to establish its divine character.

Five : Both in Calvin, and in the classical expression of Reformed theology, it becomes clear that Christian doctrine is not for its own sake, but for the sake of goodness. What supremely interested Calvin was " the pure doctrine of godliness ", that doctrine which led men to become God-like in their character and to do the will of God in their conduct. " Truth is in order to goodness ", says one of the constitutional articles of the Presbyterian Church in the U.S.A. In this affirmation the status of doctrine in Reformed theology received classical formulation. Sound doctrine is for a sound life. The ethical belongs to the essence of Christian truth. This has some very important implications. It means that the finality of Christian doctrine can never be purely speculative. Reformed thinkers are not interested in prying open the secrets of the universe in order to indulge a merely speculative bent. They theologize in order that the divine truth may be more perfectly known, so that in turn the divine will may be more perfectly obeyed. Reformed theology is equally untrue to its nature when it pursues logomachy, and becomes immersed in controversies over words or about things with respect to which there is no Biblical authority. Nor dare it confine its energies to the creation of an orthodoxy for its own sake. When orthodoxy becomes a badge to be ostentatiously worn, instead of a lamp to guide our feet, a belt to brace us for life's pilgrimage, and a banner under which we militate for God's Kingdom, it becomes an emblem of self-righteous complacency and the tombstone of vital religion.

It should ever be remembered, at the same time, that, according to Reformed theology, goodness in the full Christian sense involves not only the discharge of a vocation in the Church or society; it may also involve political action. For Christians are called upon to assume responsibility under God for society and its institutions, for the state and its policies. For life in its wholeness is under God and is the sphere of His concern and action. Therefore, Christians cannot escape responsibility of a social, cultural, and political kind.

The same connection between truth and goodness may be expressed in another way. Doctrine is for the sake of religion, and not religion for the sake of doctrine. That much abused and often disdained term, " piety ", is central in Reformed theology and must be given fresh meaning as well as fresh currency. If the contention that " Truth is in order to goodness " expresses the status and finality of Christian doctrine in the Reformed system, two corollaries follow which are of great importance for the contribution of Reformed theology to the thought and life of to-day. First, it needs to be made perfectly clear that assent to the truest and purest Christian doctrine cannot be a substitute for holy living. Personal faith in the Christ who is the central theme of Christian doctrine, and a life lived in conformity with His " mind ", give the ultimate criterion of a

Christian's standing before God and men. Christian doctrine is accepted and propagated by many who, according to the New Testament standard of the inseparable connection between belief, on the one hand, and character and conduct, on the other, are pure pagans. It must be insisted with equal conviction that the dialectical situation in which man finds himself in his thinking and behaviour due to his finitude and the grim power of sin, cannot be regarded as being more ultimate than the power of the Holy Spirit and the grace of our Lord Jesus Christ. Sinful men and women who have believed upon Christ can become "more than conquerors" in every concrete situation in which they live, and amid all the tests to which they may be subjected. For "where sin abounds, grace does much more abound".

The most relevant symbol for Reformed thought and action to-day is John Calvin's crest of the flaming heart in the outstretched hand. Christian doctrine must lead in life to the warm and unreserved surrender of the heart to God, as well as to the ceaseless dedication of the hand to those good works which God requires in loyalty to His will. Only in the measure in which this symbol becomes real can theology be saved from the stigma of having led time and again to dead orthodoxy or to sterile ethicism.

Only by taking seriously this same great symbol can doctrine be saved from becoming an instrument of schism and division. No doctrine can be regarded as "pure" which does not produce pure hearts and clean hands. Only in extreme cases, when the very core of the Christian faith is affected by a proposed change in the doctrinal constitution of a Church, should the communion of saints be broken. In most instances schism and division work evil more lasting and irrevocable than disagreement over matters that do not belong to the esssential core of the Christian revelation. A passion for Christian unity is part of the Reformed heritage, the heritage that comes from a man who was the supreme ecumenical figure in the sixteenth century.

Six: Our final reflection is this: In loyalty to the genius of the Reformed theology, the Christian Church should, from time to time, revise her confession or creed. This the Church should do in order to bring her subordinate standards into closer harmony with the Word of God and that the Body of Christ, in the face of new heresies that may be spawned and new situations that may develop, may be provided with more adequate instruments for thought and behaviour. According to the great Dutch Calvinist, Abraham Kuyper, the fault of the Church has not been that she wrote creeds, but that she has ceased to write creeds. No tradition in Christian theology is more favourably situated than the Reformed, nor is any more earnestly challenged by reason of its catholicity, to take the lead in our time in the formulation of an ecumenical theology. As the years go by the fulfilment of this task becomes the principal need of Christian thinking in the twentieth century.

PART II

8

PROTESTANTISM

IT IS AN IMPRESSIVE, ALBEIT UNHAPPY, FACT THAT the Christian religion, the most influential and aggressive of the great religions of mankind, has been represented for the past four hundred years by three separate traditions, Eastern Orthodoxy, Roman Catholicism, and Protestantism. These traditions, while they all derive from a common source and profess the essential Christian loyalties, differ from one another in very basic respects.

The Christian tradition which took historical form most recently is known by the general name of Protestantism. In its institutional expression, Protestantism is the youngest of the three Christian traditions. To be more specific, it is that Christian tradition which owes its ecclesiastical form, its confessional position, its spiritual attitude to the attempt made in the sixteenth century to give a more adequate expression to Christianity than that which was current at the time. The historic endeavour to restore the Christian religion to its native, pristine glory, is commonly called the Protestant Reformation. This revolutionary movement in the field of religion became the source of a diversified expression of Christianity. Because of its variegated character, Protestantism as a phenomenon in history is difficult to define. "If we are thinking of a purely historical definition of Protestantism", says Ernest Troeltsch, " we soon recognize that for Protestantism as a whole, it cannot be immediately formulated ". From the viewpoint of its inner religious spirit, however, as distinguished from that of its outer diversified expression, Protestantism can be readily defined.

Some important facts should be held in mind as we undertake this study. While Protestantism emerged in history at a given time and under special circumstances, its ideas and spirit were not a creation of the sixteenth century. For these it claims high antiquity. It was the contention of the Protestant Reformers, and continues to be the contention of their successors, that the religious emphases that began to be made in that century were not discoveries of new truth, but rather recoveries of ancient truth. The Reformers did not regard themselves as discoverers but as restorers. They did not think of their work as opening up new paths, but as re-opening old paths, great highways of truth, which in the course of Christian history had been abandoned or grown over. Their emphasis from the beginning was positive, not negative.

The term " Protestant ", it is true, suggests, at first thought, a negative attitude. It has been interpreted as an attitude of pure dissent from a positive position. Nothing could be more untrue, historically and etymologically, to the famous " Protest " which was presented at the Diet of Spires in 1529, and which gave its name to the new religious movement. The German princes and the representatives of the fourteen free cities which had embraced the principles of the religious reform did not "protest" against ideas; they appeared in the role of "protestants" because a curb had been placed upon the free propagation of truths which were decidedly positive in character. Etymologically, moreover, "protest" means dissent only in a secondary sense. The essence of the word is to "state as a witness", to "aver", "to make solemn affirmation". As we engage, therefore, in the study of what Protestantism is, it is well that our minds be disabused of the idea that what will engage our attention is a negative dissent from a positive position. The genius of Protestant Christianity is affirmation, not negation.

We begin with a description of Protestantism from the viewpoint of history. Within the perspective of the last four centuries, Protestantism has expressed itself in two main religious types. These may be called (A) Classical Protestantism, (B) Radical Protestantism. By Classical Protestantism we mean the great churchly systems, which, while they revolted against what Christianity had become, retained a catholic sense of the Church. Classical, or churchly Protestantism, has been represented by the Lutheran, the Reformed, and the Anglican Churches. Radical Protestantism is the word used to designate the so-called "sect" phenomenon in Protestant history. It embraces religious groups and schools of religious thought which were formed around some particular emphasis, to the right or to the left, which the members of the group felt to be expressive of the essential core of Christianity.

Classical Protestantism

Classical Protestantism, toward which, it may be remarked, Protestantism as a whole is steadily moving at the present time, discovers certain common characteristics of a basic kind. Its leaders, the Reformers of the sixteenth century, proclaimed to the world that the Reform movement was not a schism from the Church, but a schism in the Church. They claimed to be heirs of the full Biblical and Patristic heritage of the Christian Church. They were not sectarians. They viewed themselves as men whom God had commissioned to fight His battles and the battles of His Church in a degenerate time. Against the authority of the Papal See, which in the medieval period had come to claim plenary jurisdiction over all Christendom, they made their appeal to Jesus Christ Himself, and to the " next free General Council of Holy Christendom ". Classical Protestantism appealed to origins against developments in Christian history. It proclaimed a once-for-allness in the redemptive activity of God, both with respect to what He did for men, and with respect to what He said to men regarding their relationship to Him. It affirmed that Christianity is primarily an individual relation of the soul to God, founded upon the once-for-all redemptive act which God wrought in Christ, and maintained by the abiding presence of the Holy Spirit in the Christian heart. It made its appeal from a religious hierarchy to Christ, from tradition to the Bible, from an ecclesiastical system to the living fellowship which the Spirit created at Pentecost.

1. *Lutheranism.* Earliest among the general expres-

sions of Classical Protestantism is Lutheranism. By Lutheranism is meant that particular Christian emphasis and those particular churches which owe their origin to the activity, spirit, and emphasis of Martin Luther. Lutheran churches are found chiefly in Germany, the Scandinavian countries, and the United States. Following their founder, they have been profoundly concerned throughout their history about two main things: the life of the soul, and the worship of the Sanctuary. Luther's agonizing concern about the problem of personal sin, his dramatic release from its fetters through the Biblical truth of justification by faith, his religious subjectivity and love of song, have left their imprint upon the Lutheran tradition.

It is the supreme function of the Church, according to the Lutheran view, to see to it that the Word of God is truly preached, and that the Sacraments are rightly administered. In the Lutheran communion, questions of polity and order have always been secondary to a concern for the preaching of the Word and the administration of the Sacraments. The individual lay Christian fulfils his function when he bears witness to God by a holy life and discharges his secular duty with a sense of religious vocation. The glory of Lutheranism lies in the spiritual inwardness it has created in its adherents. Its emphasis upon faith, liberty, and brotherly love gave rise to some of the finest expressions of Christian piety, both individual and corporate. Bach, the prince of musicians, was a child of the Lutheran tradition.

The Church has not been regarded by Lutherans as responsible for the secular order. They have consistently maintained that the attempt should not be made to apply the law of love to the realm of politics. Because of sin, the political order does not and cannot operate in accordance with the laws of God's Kingdom. In consequence of this attitude, there has grown up in Lutheranism what must be regarded as an unhappy detachment of the Church from secular society. The latter has been allowed to develop according to its own laws. The Church has not felt itself responsible to dictate to rulers or to influence state policy. It has demanded only that it be left entirely free to preach the Word and to administer the Sacraments, and that all its members shall enjoy freedom to pursue their religious life in tranquillity and peace.

While the accusation is utterly false that to Luther belongs the main responsibility for Adolf Hitler and German Nazism, it is true that the traditional detachment of Lutheranism from public affairs in Germany made it easier for society and the state in that country to pry themselves loose from Christian direction. It is, therefore, an exceedingly important fact in contemporary Protestant history that the great Lutheran Communion, both in Europe and the United States, is beginning to re-value its social responsibility.

2. *Calvinism.* Second in historical order, and first in the order of its influence and the number of its adherents in the Protestant world of to-day, is Calvinism or, as it is also called, Reformed Christianity.

Reformed Christianity originated in the work of John Calvin, whose passion was to reform existing Christianity so that it might resemble original Christianity. Calvin, a Frenchman, and the only man of his time who was the peer of Erasmus as a Humanist, passed through a profound religious experieice, as a result of which, in the words of his follower, Beza, " he renounced all other studies and devoted himself to God ". By means of his theological writings, especially *The Institutes of the Christian Religion,* and his activities as a preacher, lecturer, and church organizer in Geneva, where he settled upon his exile from France, Calvin became one of the most revolutionary figures in religious and secular annals. More than any other man in his time, he saved Europe from disaster. While the passion of Luther, the former monk, was the soul and its salvation, the passion of Calvin, the former humanist layman, was truth and a doctrine of God. He was a God-intoxicated man. Feeling himself to be heir to the whole Christian tradition, as expressed in the Bible and the great Fathers of the Church, Calvin became the architect of the most massive and potent system of theology in the history of Protestantism, the Protestant counterpart of the great *Summa* of Thomas Aquinas. Yet, significantly enough, as demonstrating Calvin's sense of continuity with the Christian past, *The Institutes,* his theological masterpiece, is essentially an extended commentary upon the Apostles' Creed. This fact reveals how closely linked Calvin felt himself to be to the historic Christian faith. He became at the same time the architect of an ecclesiastical structure which was destined to exercise a profound influence upon the political history of Europe and the Western world.

Reformed theology, following Calvin, makes several important emphases. Religion does not exist primarily for personal happiness or for public utility; it exists for the worship and service of God. It serves man best when it puts God first. The source of Christian doctrine is Holy Scripture alone, which is "the infallible rule of faith and practice". The criterion by which a doctrinal position must be judged is the influence it exercises upon life, for "truth is in order to goodness". Pure doctrine must express itself in pure living on the part of all who profess it. In the words of that compendium of Calvinistic doctrine, the Westminster Shorter Catechism, "Man's chief end is to glorify God and to enjoy Him for ever". The Christian who lives thus, develops in his life an asceticism of a very special character, an asceticism-in-the-world, which leads him to live the life of God in full contact with the secular order. This attitude determined the attitude of Calvinists towards work and public office. Calvin's crest, a flaming heart in an open hand, the oblation of personality in its wholeness to the living God for sacrificial service, constitutes the genius of the Reformed view of life. Its representation in art is Rembrandt's famous picture, "The Syndics".

Reformed Christianity has a high doctrine of the Church and of the Church's responsibility for the secular order. The Church, in Calvin's words, is "the foundation of the world". It is "the holy community which in its life must demonstrate that God has created the world in order that it may be the theatre of His glory". In its visible expression the Christian Church is made up of "the whole multitude, dispersed all over the world, who profess to worship one God and Jesus Christ, who are initiated into His faith by baptism, who testify their unity in true doctrine and character by a participation of the sacred supper, who consent to the word of the Lord, and preserve the ministry which Christ has instituted for the purpose of preaching it."[1] The government of the Church is in the hands of a presbytery, which is made up equally of ministers and laymen, ministers who are " teaching elders ", and laymen who are " ruling elders ". For Calvin, schism is the worst of all evils which can affect the Church. " Whoever departs from the Church," he said, " denies God and Jesus Christ." To the end of his days Calvin longed for the reunion of Christendom. His consistently ecumenical spirit has been reborn, as we shall see later in this study, in a rebirth of Church and ecumenical consciousness in the Protestant world of our time.

The Church, however, does not fulfil its full mission in the world as the instrument of God's glory when it is merely concerned about preaching the Word, administering the Sacraments, producing Christian piety, and carrying on its own institutional life. It has also a mission to the community. Reformed Christianity has profoundly influenced cultural, political, and social life in every country where it has been a dominant influence. In Scotland, John Knox, Calvin's great disciple, established a school alongside every Church. At the time of the American Civil War, the Presbyterian Church led all the Christian Churches in the number of colleges it had founded from the Atlantic to the Pacific. It is also worthy of note that in the American Revolution the only clergyman who signed the Declaration of Independence was John Wither-

[1] *Institutes*, IV, 17.

spoon, the Presbyterian President of the College of New Jersey, now Princeton University, and that the first ecclesiastical body to hail the new order was the Presbytery of Hanover in Virginia. It is equally notable as a fact of contemporary history, that Fascism has not appeared in any country in which Reformed Christianity was the dominant expression of religious life. The man whose influence inspired the organization of the Confessional Church in Germany was Karl Barth, the famous Reformed theologian who dared Hitler, and sounded the return to Biblical Christianity.

Calvinistic influence in thought is found historically not only in the Presbyterian or Reformed family of churches, but also in the Anglican, the Congregational, and the Baptist churches. The ecclesiastical influence of Calvinism is found in those churches whose polity has been based upon Presbytery, which in the Reformed system takes the place of the hierarchy in Episcopal churches. Reformed churches are widely scattered throughout the world, and constitute together the largest single body of Protestant Christians.

3. *Anglicanism.* The Anglican Church is the Church of England, which since the reign of Henry VIII has been the Established Church of that country. Taking historical form as a separate ecclesiastical entity, following a quarrel between Henry VIII and the Pope, the Anglican Church owes its specific character and spirit not to anything associated with the notorious English monarch or his reign but to great men like Richard Hooker and Jeremy Taylor who became the creators of Anglicanism as we know it.

PROTESTANTISM

The Anglican Church has always aspired to be, as T. S. Eliot has expressed it, "a mean between Papacy and Presbytery". This is true not only in an ecclesiastical sense but also in a doctrinal sense. Anglicanism has had, from the beginning of its separate existence, an intense sense of the Church and of its own continuity with the Church of the Apostles. This sense of the Church, "the Church of Christ which was from the beginning, is, and continues until the end", to quote the words of Richard Hooker in the second book of his *Laws of Ecclesiastical Polity*, has determined the spirit and attitude of Anglicanism throughout its history. Regarding the Church as an extension of the Incarnation, and its own role as that of mediating between the churches of the Reformation, and the great hierarchical churches whose ancient seats were at Rome and Constantinople, the Church of England has followed a *via media*. It has been, as one has put it, "a Catholic Church with prophetic elements". Its genius has not been to revolutionize but to permeate. It has sought to keep within its pale all those who profess loyalty to the Church, however different their emphases may be upon specific issues not relating to the basic Anglican allegiance. While being Calvinistic in its essential doctrine, as this is expressed in the Thirty-Nine Articles, considerations of polity and liturgy rather than considerations of doctrine have, generally speaking, determined Anglican history and decisions. Viewing Anglicanism within the general framework of Protestant doctrine and life, it might be remarked that in its theology, especially in recent times, it has laid great stress upon reason as a necessary supplement to faith. A certain asceticism and an emphasis upon the moral responsibility of the Christian to exercise self-discipline have been marks of Anglican piety.

Some further facts regarding Anglicanism are worthy of note. In full communion with the Church of England, are the Episcopal Church of Scotland and the Protestant Episcopal Church in the United States of America. From time to time, all churches belonging to the Anglican family, meet in conclave at Lambeth, England, at an ecclesiastical gathering presided over by the Archbishop of Canterbury. At this gathering decisions are made for the guidance of the Anglican Church and its affiliated communions. Within Anglicanism are found, as a matter of fact, three main groups of churchmen all of whom are equally devoted to the Church: the Evangelicals, or Low Churchmen, who stress the Gospel and the great principles of the Reformation; the Anglo-Catholics, or High Churchmen, who stress the Catholic element in the Anglican tradition, the importance of Apostolic Succession and the Real Presence in the Eucharist; the Modern Churchmen, doctrinal radicals, whose passion it is to come to terms with secular culture as represented by philosophy and science. In recent years the Church of England, particularly under the leadership of the late lamented Archbishop of Canterbury, William Temple, has given outstanding leadership in the new Ecumenical Movement and in the approach of the Church to social questions. The comprehensive character and mediating genius of Anglicanism appear in the fact that, apart from the Roman Catholic Church, the Protestant Episcopal Church in the United States was the only Christian communion which remained undivided at the close of the American Civil War.

Radical Protestantism

By Radical Protestantism we mean those Christian groups or schools of religious thought which broke away little by little from the churchly systems of Protestantism described above, or which originated independently of these. Such groups, which have varied greatly in size and importance, have constituted the "step-children of the Reformation". On the one hand, they have been nonconformist in character; on the other hand, by stressing elements in the Christian religion of vital importance for the Body of Christ, they have been not infrequently the very "salt" of Christianity. The influence of the "sect" and the "sect"—phenomenon in the history of Protestant Christianity, especially in the United States, has been of a very decisive and transforming character. At the same time it was the spectacle presented by the manifold diversity of Protestant communions, of which there are more than two hundred and fifty in the United States alone, that led the French Catholic Churchman, Bossuet, to write his famous *History of the Variations of Protestantism*. In Radical Protestantism are two main types: the Evangelical and the Humanist.

The *Evangelical type* of Radical Protestantism embraces all those Protestant groups, denominations or churches, which maintain a separate existence within the Protestant family through a sincere desire to bear witness to that kind of Christian fellowship or to that form of life or doctrine which, in the judgment of the members, conforms most closely with the will of God as revealed in Holy Scripture. Their passion has been to grasp and express in both doctrine and life the inmost meaning of Christian discipleship. Under the inspiration of this passion, there have appeared periodically in Protestant history, churches of "gathered" or committed Christians. The "gathered" church is a church whose members are what they are not because of family connections or for conventional reasons, but because of their personal commitment to Jesus Christ and to that for which the fellowship stands. The religion of the "gathered" church has been marked by a certain primitivism in a double sense. It has been elemental religion, that kind of religion, which, in the words of William James, is an "acute fever" and not a "dull habit". It has, at the same time, represented a desire to have daily life conform to the most primitive Christian pattern. In the sphere of morals, the lives of those belonging to the "gathered" church have been marked by a severe, and oftentimes legalistic, rigourism. Their sense of the Church in the classical meaning of that term has been slight. For them the Church is essentially a voluntary association.

Protestant Christians of this type have played a very decisive part in religious and political history since the Reformation. They have been used by God to keep alive certain essential elements of Christian faith and practice. In the political realm, they have played an important part, as did Roger Williams, for example, in leading the state to grant complete religious freedom to all citizens. They have been traditional champions of the rights of man. The British Labour party drew its chief support at first from the ranks of religious Nonconformism.

Most representative and important among the Evangelical expressions of Radical Protestantism have been the Baptists, the Congregationalists, the Methodists, and the Quakers.

The Baptists, who are the successors of the Anabaptists of pre-Reformation times, have stood for the necessity of personal religious commitment as the prerequisite for Christian baptism. They constitute the largest body of Protestant Christians in the United States and have been marked, especially in the South, by great evangelistic fervour.

The Congregationalists owe their separate existence to a polity which makes the individual congregation the ultimate ecclesiastical unit. Congregationalism, traditionally Calvinistic in its theology, exercised a decisive influence on the religious life of New England in colonial days and gave birth to the universities of Harvard and Yale. To-day Congregationalists are among the chief supporters of the ecumenical movement, and a considerable number of the leading theological minds in America belong to the Congregational communion. In their polity Baptists are also Congregationalists.

Methodism originated under John and Charles Wesley as a movement within Anglicanism to secure that all who called themselves Christians should take their calling seriously and live holy or sanctified lives. Methodists constitute a large and influential group in world Protestantism. More interested in life than in doctrine, Methodists have frequently taken the lead in the initiation of social reform. The largest single ecclesiastical body in Protestantism is the Methodist Church of the United States.

The Quakers, or the Society of Friends, have stood since the days of George Fox, the founder of the Society, for the reality of the inner light in the Christian soul as a source of spiritual insight and a guide to daily living. Members of the Society of Friends both in the Old World and the New have been marked traditionally by a profound human passion and social concern. In time of war they have been pacifists who devoted themselves unstintingly to alleviating suffering.

In the world of to-day all four of these denominations, which began as " gathered " churches with an intense " sect " consciousness, manifest the same inclusiveness in their membership that marked the Protestant Churches of the classical tradition.

The Humanist type of Radical Protestantism has been supremely concerned with the relation of the Christian and the Church to secular society. One of its major passions has been to vindicate Christianity to " men of taste " and to accommodate it to Reason and the most approved cultural categories. Its representatives have generally been individuals, or groups of individuals, drawn from many churches rather than whole religious bodies in the ecclesiastical sense. Turning from Revelation as the supreme guide of thought, men of this type espoused Reason as the ultimate source of truth. Maintaining that the highest role of religion is to be the soul of culture, they have aimed to fit Christianity into the prevailing cultural pattern. Their ultimate criterion of religious truth has not been the Christian revelation but some dis-

PROTESTANTISM

covery of science or some philosophical principle or value. For Protestants of this "modernist" type, the Christian Church has been little more than a sociological institution. It has been to them one of the forces, perchance the highest, "among the various spiritual and cultural forces which are working in the same general direction of the ultimate good". Some would even suggest that the Church is simply "a voluntary association for providing services on Sunday for that section of the community which chooses to take advantage of them".

This highly secularized expression of Radical Protestantism represents the most extreme aberration from the central Christian tradition for which essential Protestantism has stood and continues to stand. Within the Protestant world of to-day the influence and prestige of this secularized variety of the Protestant spirit are very markedly on the wane. It is important, however, that we take this viewpoint into account in order to obtain a clear conception of the historical range of Protestant opinion. In this way we shall be prepared for a basic study of the eternal core of Protestantism, and of the new and striking developments in the Protestant world which constitute one of the chief religious phenomena of the twentieth century.

DOCTRINAL EMPHASES

From historical description we pass to theological interpretation. It will be our endeavour in this section to express the soul of Protestant Christianity. Amid and beneath all the diverse manifestations of Protestantism in history, we discover certain major emphases which together constitute the inmost core of Protestant faith and life.

The Supreme Authority of the Bible. Protestantism emerged in history with the affirmation that the Bible, the Scriptures of the Old and New Testaments, rather than Tradition or the Church, constitutes the supreme authority in all questions relating to Christian faith and practice. This affirmation was directed against the authority of the Roman Catholic Church, particularly the Papacy, which had vested in itself the authority formerly exercised by the Ecumenical Councils. The Protestant Reformers proclaimed that authoritative knowledge of God and His will is derived from a study of Holy Scripture. The Bible, which in the medieval Church had existed only in a Latin version, was now translated from the original Hebrew and Greek into the several languages of the West. It soon began to be studied not only by churchmen and scholars but also by the common people. The presupposition that underlay the translation of the Scriptures into the vernacular tongues of Europe, and later of the whole world, was and continues to be, that the Holy Spirit, under whose inspiration the writers of the sacred Record had done their work, would lead humble souls to a saving knowledge of God. Tradition, which had come to be regarded as coequal in authority with the Bible as a source of our knowledge of God, and the Church, which had become the proximate rule of faith and the supreme interpreter of Revelation, were now studied and judged in the light of the Bible.

The restoration of the Bible to the supreme place

of religious authority which it had occupied in the early Church has had far-reaching implications for Protestant thought and life. One implication touches the meaning of Divine Revelation. The classical Christian affirmation is that God has spoken. The eternal silence has been broken. The inscrutable mystery has been unveiled. There is a word from the Lord. Truth exists. This truth is redemptive truth. It has taken the form of great redemptive deeds wrought by God in behalf of man, and of luminous prophetic words which interpreted those deeds and made clear to man the nature and will of God for his salvation. The record of those deeds and words we have in the Bible. The core of the Bible and the clue to its understanding is the Gospel. The Gospel is the Good News of what God has already done for man in Christ, and is ready to do for any person who believes the record concerning Jesus Christ, the Saviour. They only, however, really understand the Bible and attain a knowledge of God and His redemptive will who come to the study of Holy Scripture not because of intellectual curiosity but through a deep concern to discover authoritative answers to the agonizing questions about God, sin, and destiny.

Biblical truth is, moreover, personal truth. Being a book about redemption, the Bible is supremely interested in answering the quest of a person who comes to it with the query, " What must I do to be saved? " This question is answered in the form of an encounter between God and the earnest reader in such wise that the centuries are telescoped, and a redemptive encounter takes place again. Not only so: from the hour of the great encounter onward, it is in and through the Bible that the Christian soul holds communion with God. Through the Bible also, the will of God is revealed to the Christian for his behaviour in the concrete process of living. The Bible is, therefore, not only the supreme source of our knowledge of God and the supreme theatre where God and man meet; it is also the chief medium of our communion with God and the chief guide in the proper conduct of life.

As regards an understanding of Biblical truth, the Bible is to be interpreted in terms of categories which are native to itself. Being a book about redemption, that is to say, about the supernatural disclosure of God to men as a redeeming God, the Bible cannot be understood in terms of any categories and forms of thought which are alien to the basic presupposition that God revealed Himself in a redemptive manner in the life of Israel. Basic for a true understanding of the Bible is the recognition, for example, that one of its central categories is that of a " covenant " between God and His people whereby He promises to bless them and they promise to do His Will. Moreover, being a book about redemption, the Bible is authoritative only in its own particular sphere. As a document with a history, it is to be studied and investigated with the most rigorous historical and scientific criteria. Under such scrutiny, a flood of light has been thrown upon the origin of the Biblical records, as also upon the elements that entered into Israel's religion. The important thing about the Bible is, however, that whereas the human, often all too human, elements are abundantly present, God used lowly and unworthy people and religious elements of a plebeian and even exotic character, to communicate Himself and His purpose to men. His self-communication moved progressively from the early origins of Israel's history through the great prophets of Israel and Judah, took personal and absolute form in Jesus Christ, and was perfected in the Apostolic era of the Spirit. Revelation as a whole is bound together by the central reality of the Redeemer, so that there is a sense in which one can call the Bible a book about Jesus Christ. It is in the measure in which He becomes known in His saving power that the Bible becomes truly understood. While it is not true that the Bible is the " religion of Protestants ", as has sometimes been said, it is true that the Bible produced the Protestant Reformation and has inspired and determined the Protestant expression of the Christian religion.

The centrality given to the Bible in Protestant faith and experience exerted a profound influence upon those forms of cultural development which are Protestant in their inspiration. Popular interest in the Bible gave a great impulse to public education. Literacy was promoted in order that men might learn to read the Scriptures. Where the Bible has been diffused, the common people have become literate, while culture in every sphere has been transfigured. In many instances the Bible itself was the first book to be translated into the language of a people. In other instances, a particular translation of the Bible gave classical expression to the language in which it appeared. The great figures, episodes, and teachings of the Book have entered as a creative force into the main stream of many a literature. It is a striking and symbolical fact that Rembrandt and Bach, two of the greatest masters in the history of art, one in painting, the other in music, were Protestants, and that their greatest creations were directly inspired by the text of Holy Scripture. Both men were profound students of the Bible whose inner meaning they succeeded in interpreting in a way that no other artists have ever done.

The Unmediated Lordship of Jesus Christ. The centrality of Christ in Christian thought and experience, and the unmediated character of relations between Him and the souls of men, is a basic Protestant emphasis. Jesus Christ does not submit to control or patronage even by the Church, as the Grand Inquisitor in Dostoïevski's famous legend thought he should. He maintains Himself in sovereign freedom, using the Church as the agent of His will, but bringing it into judgment when it becomes presumptuous and assumes prerogatives which Christ has never relinquished. A fourfold affirmation makes up the Protestant insight into the meaning and significance of Jesus Christ and His relations with men.

1. *Salvation is obtained through faith in Jesus Christ.* The doctrine of Justification by Faith has been called the formal principal of Protestantism. Its meaning is this: Man is saved, not by ethical striving or achievement, but by the joyous acceptance of God's gift of salvation. Good works do not save men; they are the fruits of men who are saved. God offers to man the complete redemption which was wrought out for him in the life, death, and resurrection of Jesus Christ. To the reality of this redemption, man gives his assent, asquiescing in the fact that he owes salvation not to his own goodness, but to the goodness of

Another. By an act of consent or commitment, he gives himself to that Other, the living Christ, with whom he identifies himself in thought and in life. In this view of faith there are, accordingly, two elements: one, the element of assent by which the mind grasps and acquiesces in what God has done for men in Christ; the other, that of consent or commitment, whereby a man identifies himself wholly with Christ in thought and in life. In saving faith, therefore, there is assent to a proposition, and consent to a Person.

Believers in Christ, whoever they may be, enter upon a life of unique privilege and responsibility. They are constituted "priests". As such they have full right or access to God through Christ at all times. It is their corresponding responsibility to live lives of utter dedication to God, in the secular as well as in the religious sphere. The doctrine of the "universal priesthood of believers" is a basic Protestant affirmation.

2. *Jesus Christ is the sovereign Lord of the Church and of the World.* While affirming that Jesus Christ founded a Church which is His Body, and that outside this Church there is no salvation, Protestantism affirms that Jesus Christ has not abdicated. He continues to direct affairs in the Church and in the world. As the Lord of the Church, he can bring and does bring the Church into judgment. That being so, a Church that bears the Christian name may so far depart from the mind of Christ in faith and practice, as virtually to become apostate and to be, in the words directed by the Lord of the Church to one of the churches in the Apocalypse, "spewed out" of His mouth. It means also that there may be times when

an individual Christian may have to appeal to Jesus Christ against the Church. This is the significance of the famous words of Pascal when he said: "If my letters are condemned in Rome, what I condemn in them is condemned in heaven: to Thy tribunal, Oh Lord Jesus, I appeal." That was the profoundly Protestant affirmation of a great Roman Catholic saint. It was in the spirit of that affirmation that the Protestant Reformers made their appeal to Jesus Christ Himself against those who carried on the affairs of the Church in His name.

Jesus Christ should be equally sovereign in the affairs of the state. It is never legitimate for Protestants to make any pact with, or derive special advantages from, a form of government whose principles run counter to the truths of the Christian religion, or which challenges the right of the Church to proclaim God's truth and to live in accordance with His will.

3. A third affirmation is this. *The concrete figure of Jesus Christ as He appears in the Gospels, is the normative standard for human life.* Whenever, as has frequently happened in Roman, Orthodox, and Protestant circles, the way of life and thought which was characteristic of the historical figure of Jesus is not taken seriously, the quality of Christian living immediately declines. The so-called "Back to Jesus" movement, and that of the "Quest of the historical Jesus", which were Protestant in their inspiration, despite all the great limitations attaching to this approach, gave to the Christian Church the concrete living figure of Jesus in a form in which the Church had never possessed Him before. That Figure, divested of the elements that belonged merely to His own age,

sets before each succeeding generation of men a concrete and authoritative standard of human behaviour. While it is true that Lives of Christ have been rather autobiographies of their authors than biographies of Jesus, they do enshrine the eternal truth that the most important thing that any man can do is to face the Man and to order his life in accordance with the life of Christ.

4. The fourth affirmation regarding Jesus Christ is: *the Risen Christ is the perennial source of strength for action.* Protestant piety has stressed the reality of communion with the living Christ, not only on the part of great saints but also on the part of simple believers; not only in the sacrament of the Lord's Supper but amid the routine of daily living. " Lo I am with you alway, even unto the ends of the world," said Christ. These are the words which David Livingstone called the " words of a gentleman ". A sense of comradeship with the living Christ, to whom one can go at all times for forgiveness and cleansing, for sympathy and for strength, has been one of the chief marks and sources of inspiration of Protestant Christian personality. Because of the overwhelming fact of Christ as the ever present and living Lord, Protestant Christians have not been aware of any necessity to have recourse to the Virgin Mother or to the saints as special intercessors. Having the living Lord himself, they have felt the need of no other. This Christo-centric character of religious experience amid the routine of daily living and in all the great crises of life has been a characteristic of Protestant Christianity.

The Witnessing Responsibility of the Church. The

supreme function of the Christian Church is, in the Protestant view, to bear witness to God. The Church exists to witness to the Gospel, the Good News of human salvation in and through Jesus Christ. Whenever the Church, as the "Body of Christ", thinks and acts as if it were an end in itself, or engages in activities in which the reality of the Gospel does not hold a central position, it fails to fulfil its primary function.

Witness must be borne to the Gospel by word and by life. The centrality of preaching, of proclaiming the Gospel by word, has been one of the chief characteristics of Protestant Christianity. Ideally speaking, the Gospel must be proclaimed with passionate conviction: with conviction because it is true, with passion because it is important and because obedience to it is urgent. It must be proclaimed also with unmistakable clarity in the language of every people. Clarity in the proclamation of the Gospel involves a thorough knowledge of the Bible where such knowledge is obtained; personal experience of the power of the Gospel; an adequate theological system in which the Gospel is central. The form of speech used in proclamation must be such as to convey the significance of the Good News in the most compelling form. The heart of man and the culture of the time must be assiduously studied in order that communication may take place in such a way as to be challenging and luminous.

It is for the Church also to bear witness to the Gospel by life. No witness will be more effective than that of personal piety, of spiritual inwardness, of victorious living, on the part of those who profess the name of Jesus Christ. But witness must be borne no less by a deep human or social passion. If men are to take seriously the presentation of the Good News about God, goodness must validate the presence of truth; good works must prove the reality of faith. However, personal ethical behaviour and Christian philanthropy are not enough. The Christian Church must proclaim God's righteousness for all human relationships, and must throw its weight at all times upon the side of righteousness.

Everything which the Church does in bearing witness to the Gospel by word and by life must have as its principal aim that individuals and communities may respond to the call of God. In order to exist truly, the Church, in accordance with the inner meaning of the term "exist", must "set out", "sally forth", along the highways of life, bearing witness before all men, in every circumstance and in every age, to the Good News that God has given a definite and final answer to the agonizing problems of man's life.

Contemporary Developments

We have now come to the most important part of this study, a consideration of the developments that are taking place in Protestant Christianity in our time. For Protestantism, let it be emphasized, has not yet reached its religious majority, nor discharged its full historical mission. It is still in process of becoming; its heyday is not behind it, but before it. The complete meaning of what happened at the Reformation four hundred years ago has still to be expressed in life and doctrine and ecclesiastical organization. Other things, too, must happen which did not enter into the thought of the Reformers.

That Protestant Christianity is crossing the threshold of a new era in its history is abundantly clear. It is rediscovering its soul. Protestant Churches are becoming increasingly aware of the greatness of their heritage from the past. The glory of the Gospel and its implications for the world have captivated afresh the Protestant imagination. A sense of contemporary mission is deepening. Contact has been established with the Eastern Orthodox Church. The Roman Catholic doctrine of the Church and the bearing of its pretensions upon the future of Christian unity, is being studied afresh, and from a fresh point of view. The expansion of Evangelical Christianity into every representative area of the world and the coming, in consequence, of a world-wide Evangelical community, has given a new sense of ecumenicity. The global character of contemporary problems, the physical unity of the world and its tragic spiritual disunity, constitute a new challenge to Evangelical action. The connection between human welfare and the religion prevalent in a given country has come up for new study. The devastating effects of religious monopoly and the suppression of religious freedom in large areas of the world, not only in countries where non-Christian religions have prevailed but even in others where the dominant religion has been Christian, have made a profound impression upon the Protestant mind. At the same time, there is much sober reflection upon the fact that the nations which proved victorious in the recent world struggle and which will have to assume a major responsibility for the world of to-morrow, are nations whose religious background has been predominantly Protestant or Orthodox.

Four major developments have been taking place in Protestantism in recent years which will have a far-reaching influence upon the history of Christianity and the future of human civilization. Let us state what these are and pass on to consider each one of them in turn. First: The meaning of the historic Christian faith is being grasped afresh. Second: The reality of the Holy Catholic Church, the *Una Sancta*, and its implications for the Christian community and the family of nations, has caught the Protestant imagination. Third: A reawakened sense of responsibility for the secular order inspires a passion for a new *Corpus Christianum*. Fourth: The formulation of an ecumenical theology, made necessary by the world-wide expansion of Evangelical Christianity and the new problems of culture and civilization, is being initiated by Protestant thinkers.

The Rediscovery of Christian Orthodoxy. After a sombre period during which it appeared as if Protestant theology was to succumb completely to a liberalism whose assumptions were derived from Reason rather than from Revelation, a powerful reaction has set in. The way was prepared for a renaissance of orthodoxy by the study of certain thinkers who had been largely passed by. The discussions of Pascal and Kierkegaard on the nature of Truth and of Christian truth in particular; the devastating critique of man and human nature by Dostoïevski and Nietzsche disposed men's minds to take seriously the realism of the Bible. God became greater and more transcendent; man became meaner and more problematical. The religious romanticism which had immersed God in nature and divinized man received a shattering blow when in 1918 Karl Barth, a Swiss country pastor, published a commentary on Paul's Letter to the Romans. The number of allusions to Kierkegaard, Dostoïevski and Nietzsche in this epoch-making book show how those thinkers had prepared the soul of Barth to listen with fresh understanding to the powerful voice of Paul as he spoke again to Western religion and culture. Once more the transcendence of God became real in the high places of Protestant theology; the Word of God became potent and authoritative once again; the gulf between God and man, between sin and righteousness, between truth and falsehood, between perdition and salvation, became apparent; while the Bible as the written Word, and Jesus Christ as the personal Word of God, took on new meaning. The tremendous fact was brought home to thinkers that when God speaks, the content of His word is not information to satisfy man's curiosity but a command that summons him to obedience. The inner meaning of religion, as a total response of human personality to God, became clear. The impossibility of understanding the Bible without taking up the adventurous attitude which the Bible demands, also became manifest. Existential theology, that is, theology grounded upon man's total response to God, as against religious romanticism which rooted Christianity in pure feeling, and Protestant scholasticism which reduced it to the mere acceptance of theological formulas and the

Biblical letter, had arrived. While so-called Barthianism has few adherents in its original form, and Karl Barth himself refuses to be known as a Barthian, the diffused influence of this German Swiss theologian and of his compatriot Emil Brunner has led to a rebirth of Protestant orthodoxy. That influence may be traced in many thinkers, both Protestant and Roman Catholic, who differ from these two theologians in many respects.

The appearance of a theological commentary on a book of the Bible, as distinguished from a merely critical and historical discussion, was soon followed by a new interest in theology itself. In the Protestant world, theology in general, and systematic theology in particular, had largely fallen into disrepute. Not doctrine but life was the prevailing slogan. The content of theology was determined largely by psychology or sociology, by philosophy or the history of religion. Now the Bible and the Bible alone became the supreme source of theology, as it had been in the Protestant tradition when it first broke upon the world. A new Biblicism was born which, while eager to do the fullest justice to the authenticated results of literary and historical criticism as applied to the Biblical records, was still prepared to affirm with intellectual conviction and passionate faith that the Bible was the Word of God to man. The Record of God's Self-disclosure in redemptive deed and prophetic word, in the person and work of Jesus Christ, in the coming of the Holy Spirit and the creation of the Christian Church, was where God and man supremely met. In the theological construction now undertaken of the doctrine of the person of Christ were blended the Jesus of history and the Christ of Paul, the Word become flesh of the Fourth Gospel and the King of Kings and Lord of Lords of the Apocalypse. The Old Testament soon began to be studied with fresh eyes not as a mere preface to, but as an integral part of, the Christian revelation. Fresh attention was given to the writings of Luther and Calvin and the other great Reformers of the sixteenth century. As a result of this study it was discovered that some of the greatest insights of those great men had been lost or dimmed in the Protestant theology of the succeeding period. When the white light of Revelation was turned upon the study of man and the human scene, it became evident that man was chiefly distinguished from the animals not only by his rationality, but also, and very especially, by his " capacity for self-deception ". His characteristic sin was no longer lust, but rebellious pride. His supreme sin, to which he was constantly subject, was to substitute himself or something else for God, his Maker. Thus, in the higher spheres of Protestant theology, a new Christian realism was born. It was also proclaimed once more that the glory of the Christian preacher was to be a " servant of the Word ".

In the period between the two wars, and under the double inspiration of the reborn interest in Christian orthodoxy and the growing desire for Christian understanding and unity, two great gatherings were convened. The object of the one was to crystallize Christian truth for the churches which professed it. One of the chief objects of the other was to define the Christian message in relation to the non-Christian religions. The first of these gatherings, called the

Conference on Faith and Order, was held at Lausanne, Switzerland, in 1927. The second, an enlarged meeting of the International Missionary Council, assembled for two weeks on the Mount of Olives at Easter time, 1928, to consider the relation of Christianity to the non-Christian religions and the world of our time. Out of the Jerusalem gathering, and under the inspiration of what had taken place at Lausanne the year before, there came forth, in the form of a message, one of the great documents of contemporary Christianity. In the intervening two decades the Jerusalem message has exercised a wide and consolidating influence upon Protestant thought throughout the world. To make clear what is believed in the higher circles of Protestant leadership to-day, we can do no better than to quote part of this document. The chairman of the commission which drafted the message was the Archbishop of Canterbury, William Temple. The message reads in part: "Our message is Jesus Christ. He is the revelation of what God is and of what man through Him may become. In Him we come face to face with the Ultimate Reality of the universe; He makes known to us God as our Father, perfect and infinite in love and in righteousness; for in Him we find God incarnate, the final yet ever-unfolding, revelation of the God in whom we live and move and have our being.

"We hold that through all that happens, in light and in darkness, God is working, ruling and overruling. Jesus Christ, in His life and through His death and resurrection, has disclosed to us the Father, the Supreme Reality, as almighty Love, reconciling the world to Himself by the Cross, suffering with men in their struggle against sin and evil, bearing with them and for them the burden of sin, forgiving them as they, with forgiveness in their own heart, turn to Him in repentance and faith, and creating humanity anew for an ever-growing, ever-enlarging, everlasting life.

"The vision of God in Christ brings and deepens the sense of sin and guilt. We are not worthy of His love; we have by our own fault opposed His holy will. Yet that same vision which brings the sense of guilt brings also the assurance of pardon, if only we yield ourselves in faith to the spirit of Christ so that His redeeming love may avail to reconcile us to God.

"We re-affirm that God, as Jesus Christ has revealed Him, requires all His children, in all circumstances, at all times, and in all human relationships, to live in love and righteousness for His glory. By the resurrection of Christ and the gift of the Holy Spirit He offers His own power to men that they may be fellow workers with Him, and urges them on to a life of adventure and self-sacrifice in preparation for the coming of His Kingdom in its fullness. . . .

"Christianity is not a Western religion, nor is it yet effectively accepted by the Western world as a whole. Christ belongs to the peoples of Africa and Asia as much as to the European or American. We call all men to equal fellowship in Him. But to come to Him is always self-surrender. We must not come in the pride of national heritage or religious tradition; he who would enter the Kingdom of God must become as a little child, though in that Kingdom are all the treasures of man's aspirations, consecrated and harmonized. Just because Christ is the self-disclosure of the One God, all human aspirations are towards Him, and yet of no human tradition is He merely the continuation. He is the desire of all nations; but He is always more, and other, than they had desired before they learned of Him ".[1]

The Affirmation of Evangelical Catholicity. A new sense of the Church and its universality has also been born in recent years within the representative Protestant communions. The Church within the churches becomes more and more the object of thought and devotion. A deeper study of the New Testament, and especially the restoration of the Pauline letters and the other Apostolic writings to their true place within the Christian revelation, has focused upon the Church the attention which in the liberal era of Protestantism had been focused almost exclusively upon the Kingdom of God. The eschatological character of the Kingdom has been grasped afresh. It is recognized that the Christian Church is " the pillar and ground of the truth ", that it is "the Body of Christ ", God's chosen instrument for the doing of His will in history, which must dedicate itself to the coming of His Kingdom among men. This Church came to birth as a fellowship before it became an organization. Its birth was due not to the " consenting wills of men ", but to the power of God. Being the creation of the Holy Spirit, the Church is indwelt by the Spirit and must ever strive to maintain the unity of the Spirit.

The last two decades of Protestant history have

[1] *The Jerusalem Meeting of the International Missionary Council*, International Missionary Council, New York, 1928, Vol. I, pp. 402, 411.

been marked by increasing devotion upon the part of Protestant church leaders to the cause of Christian unity. They are committed to the proposition that only a united Church can fulfil the will of Christ as expressed in His great High Priestly prayer (St. John 17) and discharge its true mission in the world. Christ Himself is the centre of unity. Allegiance to Him as Divine Saviour and Lord is the bond that binds together the several Church councils that have been formed in recent years, such as, for example, the Federal Council of the Churches of Christ in America, and the World Council of Churches. A wholehearted recognition of Christ's deity is the basis of the new Christian unity that is being sought to-day in the Protestant world. This does not mean, of course, that the goal proposed in a single ecclesiastical structure made up of all the Protestant churches in any given country, or of a world Church with a single centralized authority. Seriously to entertain such an idea would run counter to the mind of Christ and to the true meaning and structure of the Christian Church, as these are expressed in the New Testament and in the early centuries of Christian history. What is sought is a federated expression of Christianity in which an increasing number of churches would unite organically, while others would manifest a growing unity in their doctrine, life, and practical endeavour, and in their strategy with respect to the secular order.

Thus schism and division are more and more regarded as evils by the great churches that make up the Protestant family. These Churches, however, are not disposed to admit that the historical division of

Protestantism into a multiplicity of denominations has been an unmitigated evil. It is freely recognized that Protestant denominational history has many lamentable chapters in its annals. It is equally realized that the Spirit of God has used the witness and work of the great Protestant communions to set forth and to keep alive certain expressions of Christian faith and life that would otherwise have been passed over. The ecclesiastical unity now being sought is one in which each denomination, having studied itself in the light of Holy Scripture, in the light of other Christian denominations and traditions, in the light of its own history and mission, and in the light of contemporary need, shall slough off everything attaching to it which does not belong to the essence of the Christian religion, while it brings the rest, as its particular contribution, into the unity of the Body of Christ. An epoch-making step has been taken in the Protestant world when division is regarded as one of the greatest evils which can afflict the Church of Christ. In the light of Christ and the developing unity which brings the Protestant churches of the world together, schism has a hideous face. And what is the soul of schism but that any one institutional expression of the Church of Christ should presume to be the whole? Those Christians are schismatics in the worst sense who, in spite of the New Testament record and the testimony of history, regard the particular organization to which they belong as *The Church.*

Coincident with a deepened apprehension of the meaning of the Church, and an awakened passion for Christian unity, there has grown up in the Protestant world a new concept of catholicity. The nineteenth century and the first decades of the twentieth witnessed a missionary movement of the Protestant churches unparalleled in all Christian history. As a result of that movement, evangelical missions and national evangelical churches are found to-day in every representative area of the world. Soldiers, sailors, and airmen recently serving in continental areas and in remote islands of the Pacific ocean found that "The Church Was There". In this way the new vision of the Church, derived from a deepened study of the New Testament, has been paralleled on the plane of contemporary history by an expanded vision of the World Church. The Ecumenical Church, that is to say, the Church which is co-extensive with the inhabited globe, has appeared for the first time in Christian history. Its advent took place just at the time that civilization was entering upon its global era, when in a world that had achieved unprecedented physical unity abysmal spiritual rifts were forming and the earth was about to become devastated by global war. There is no more striking fact in the dramatic annals of the Christian Church than the circumstance that, during the years preceding the outbreak of the Second World War, great ecumenical gatherings were held in Europe and Asia, which were attended by the representatives of all races and of more Christian denominations than had ever come together before in all Christian history. Out of these gatherings there emerged a sense of the living reality of the Church Universal. At Jerusalem, at Oxford, at Edinburgh, at Madras, at Amsterdam, at Utrecht, a new concept of catholicity became real in experience and began to be formulated in thought.

To understand the meaning and grasp the implications of the new concept of catholicity which has emerged in the Protestant world is to take cognizance of the most significant single phenomenon in the contemporary history of Christianity. In a recent article published in the theological quarterly, *Theology Today*,[1] and entitled "The Growing Concept of Catholicity", the Church historian, Dr. Kenneth Latourette of Yale University, compares the traditionally Roman concept of catholicity with the emergent Protestant concept. To that admirable article of the great Church historian some reflections may be added. Evangelical catholicity does not confine the frontiers of the Christian Church to the boundaries of any one Christian institution. Taking seriously the great dictum that comes down to us from the Patristic era, *Ubi Christus ibi Ecclesia*, "Where Christ is, there is the Church", it considers that any Christian group that gives full allegiance to Jesus Christ in its doctrine and bears His marks in the life and witness of its members, gives unmistakable evidence of the fruits of the Holy Spirit, and so belongs to the Holy Catholic Church. Its members may have to clarify their thinking and learn the way of the Lord more perfectly, but if they give evidence of the basic Christian loyalties in faith and practice, Christ's seal is upon them and they belong to His Church. Evangelical catholicity, therefore, embraces all those, whatever their name or sign, who pledge their loyalty to Jesus Christ and manifest the fruits of the Spirit. All such are members of the Holy Catholic Church and are invited to form part of

[1] Vol. II, No. 1 (April 1945), pp. 69-76.

the ecumenical fellowship of Christian believers. They are urged to manifest their unity in Christ, to join in giving more perfect expression in thought and life to the Christian faith and its implications for the human situation, and to develop a common strategy in approaching the world and its problems. The affirmation that underlies Evangelical Catholicity is therefore this: Jesus Christ Himself, by the faith and life which He creates in those who profess to be His disciples, ultimately determines who belong to the Holy Catholic Church.

The coming of the Church Universal in concept and in reality has given birth in Protestant circles to a new science, the science of ecumenics. Ecumenics is the science of the Church Universal conceived as a world missionary community, its functions, relations, and strategy. It corresponds in the religious sphere to geopolitics in the secular. Henceforth the Christian Church in its Protestant expression will devote increasing attention to the formulation of an adequate Christian approach to the diverse problems which confront the Christian religion at the present time.

Reawakened Concern for the Secular Order. At the close of the First World War, several movements appeared among the Protestant Churches to bring the message and influence of Christianity to bear upon the life of the world. Two of these were the World Church Movement, which was organized in the United States, and the Life and Work Movement, which was international in character. The latter held a great congress at Stockholm in 1925. Both movements did their work under the influence of the idea that the lights of the coming Kingdom of God were already flushing the contemporary horizon. The churches of that time lacked a sufficiently deep insight into the realities of human nature and of the human situation. What was more, they lacked an adequate grasp of the meaning of the Church and of the great Christian verities. Under the influence of religious romanticism they felt that the transformation of human society could be accomplished if only the Church organized itself adequately for the task.

In the intervening years, the international situation grew worse. Theological insight was deepened; the nature and mission of the Church became clearer. At Oxford in July, 1937, there came together representatives of the Protestant and Eastern Orthodox Churches. Members of the clergy and eminent members of the laity were there. At a time when it began to appear that a new world war was inevitable, the members of the Church Universal assembled at Oxford, spent two weeks on issues relating to "Church, Community, and State". Out of that gathering came the slogan which has since resounded around the world: " Let the Church be the Church ".

The Oxford Conference, which grasped and formulated the true mission of the Church in the world, faced also, and in a constructive way, the Church's relationship to the whole secular order. The problem of a *Corpus Christianum* became real again. How could human society as a whole be brought under the decisive influence of Christian principles and a Christian way of living?

In the years since this decisive gathering was

held, the problems of the secular order have been envisaged with great clarity, in their social, cultural, and political aspects. Protestant leaders proclaim afresh that it is not enough to formulate ethical principles for society, nor yet to regenerate individuals through the preaching of the Gospel. It is necessary, in addition, that Christians should live out in communal form the new meaning of a true Christian life within the diverse spheres that make up Society. In other words, the true meaning of community must be correctly worked out within the representative areas of social life. As regards the cultural sphere it is pointed out that modern culture has become largely rootless. It lacks, besides, a great luminous idea to give life meaning, direction and propulsive power. The great insights of the Christian religion must therefore be given to modern culture. The question is raised afresh in Protestant circles as to the place of religion in public education. God must come again into education; reverence must be taught to youth. The Bible and the great sources of spiritual renewal must be made available for popular study.

In the sphere of politics, and especially in the sphere of international relations, a decisive influence has been exerted in the United States by the commission entitled, The Commission to Study the Bases of a Just and Durable Peace. This commission, sponsored by the Federal Council of the Churches of Christ in America, and under the chairmanship of a distinguished Protestant layman, John Foster Dulles, who received a vision of the Church and its possibilities at the Oxford Conference, has been more influential in shaping Christian public opinion in influencing the international policy of the government, than any single group in recent times that has faced the problems of peace and world order.

Now that the war is over, and the full meaning of the Ecumenical Church becomes more apparent, Protestant Christianity looks forward to bringing the insights and inspiration of Christianity to bear on the secular order with a sense of responsibility unmatched since the great schism divided the Christian Church in the West.

A Demand for an Ecumenical Theology. The new orthodoxy that takes shape in the Protestant mind, the new catholicity that inspires its ecclesiastical outlook, the Christian concern for the human situation in its global aspects that mark the Protestant Churches of to-day combine to create a longing for an authoritative Ecumenical Council. This was what the Reformers of the sixteenth century desired above anything else, " the next free general Council of Holy Christendom ", and of which they were defrauded in their time by the action of the Council of Trent in 1546. An invitation to such a council will undoubtedly be issued in due course " to all whom it may concern ". One of the chief tasks of the new Ecumenical Council will be the formulation of an ecumenical theology. Such a theology, grounded upon Holy Scripture as the supreme source of Christian doctrine, will take cognizance of the light that has fallen upon the Christian revelation under the influence of the Holy Spirit from the first century to the present. It will take account of the global character of human life to-day, and of the existence and problems of a world-wide Church in a global era. It will formulate Christian truth in relation to the new heresies which have been spawned in our time. The writer may be permitted at this point to reproduce a statement which he recently prepared on this subject and which has appeared elsewhere.[1]

Taking seriously the presence of the Holy Spirit in the Church and realizing that there is no better commentary upon the meaning of both than the history of the Church, ecumenical theology will study the Churches of the great dispersion in the light of the Bible and of Jesus Christ. Now that the Church is co-extensive with the inhabited globe, the hour has arrived to survey afresh the whole course of Church history. Let each Church in the three great traditions, Roman, Eastern, and Protestant, be studied for the witness it has borne to Christ in the course of its life, whether in the nurture of saints, the elucidation or defence of truth, or in its contribution to the effective reign of God among men. Let it be surveyed to discover whatever stains of sin, or marks of shame and error, its history may reveal. Such a study will show that no Church in history can claim a monopoly of insight or sainthood, of evangelical zeal or transforming power. Those things which God has taught the Church through the glory and shame of the churches will provide data for an ecumenical theology. A theology of Revelation, which cherishes without idolatry the historic Creeds and Confessions, which studies the life history of the churches in search of insight regarding Christ and the Church, which embraces within its sweep God's dealing with the new

[1] "The Times Call for Theology," *Theology Today*, Vol. II, No. 1 (April 1945), pp. 7 and 5.

Churches in Asia, Africa, Oceania and Latin America can lay the foundation of that theology which is needed by an Ecumenical Church in an ecumenical world.

Let the Churches of the Reformation acknowledge their many sins and shortcomings, admitting freely that the Church can sin and has sinned. In penitence and humility, in faith and in hope, let them prepare for the tasks that await them in the coming time. And about one thing let them be quite clear. The theological statement to which the Church Universal must look forward in the years ahead must be no doctrinal syncretism or theological dilution. It must have at the heart of it no pale, lowest denominator formula. Never must the Church sponsor a blanched, eviscerated, spineless statement of confessional theology. It must give birth in this revolutionary, transition time, to a full blooded, loyally Biblical, unashamedly ecumenical, and strongly vertebrate system of Christian belief.

SELECTED BIBLIOGRAPHY

Protestantism. By William Ralph Inge. London, 1928.
A Compend of Calvin's Institutes, Philadelphia, 1939;
A Compend of Luther's Theology, Philadelphia, 1943. Edited by Hugh Thomson Kerr, Jr.
The Christian Message in a Non-Christian World. By Hendrik Kraemer. New York, 1938.
History of the Expansion of Christianity. By Kenneth L. Latourette. 7 vols. New York, 1937–1945.
A Preface to Christian Theology. New York, 1941. By John A. Mackay, editor, *Theology Today,* Princeton, New Jersey.
Unitive Protestantism. By John Thomas McNeill. New York, 1930.

The Nature and Destiny of Man. By Reinhold Niebuhr. 2 vols. New York, 1941–1943.
Romanism and Evangelical Christianity. By E. J. Paul. London, 1940.
The Vitality of the Christian Faith. Edited by George F. Thomas. New York, 1944.
Protestantism and Progress. By Ernst Troeltsch, translated by W. Montgomery. New York, 1912.
The Conference on Church, Community, and State: J. H. Oldham, *The Oxford Conference, Official Report,* Chicago, 1937; W. A. Visser 'tHooft and J. H. Oldham, *The Church and Its Function in Society,* Chicago, 1937.
Man's Disorder and God's Design. The Amsterdam Assembly Series.

9

AS REGARDS FREEDOM OF RELIGION

A BOOK WAS PUBLISHED RECENTLY ENTITLED, *Religious Liberty: An Inquiry*.[1] Its author is M. Searle Bates, Professor of History, Nanking University. In a volume of six hundred pages the author has focused the problem of religious liberty with a comprehensiveness, a pointedness, and a fairness of judgment which make the product of his research and reflection a classic contribution to the field which it covers. Nothing just like this study has ever been attempted, and the book will long remain a standard volume on the subject with which it deals. No thoughtful minister or layman should fail to read this volume and keep it by him as a source book for constant reference.

Referring to Dr. Bates's book a distinguished Roman Catholic scholar, the Reverend John Courtney Murray, S.J., has expressed himself in these terms: " Among all the problems relating to a new world order, religious liberty occupies a unique position. The reason is, no other problem so directly and immediately faces an ultimate issue."[2] The appear-

[1] Published for the International Missionary Council by Harper Brothers.
[2] *Theological Studies*, March 1945.

ance of the "Inquiry" and this comment by Dr. Murray provide an occasion for some reflections upon the supremely important topic of freedom of religion.

It is impossible to discuss religious freedom without clarifying first of all the concept of freedom in general. What is freedom? When can it be said that a man is free? A man is free when he gives voluntary allegiance to something that is greater than himself or his own self interest. Merely to be free from something or someone is an empty abstraction. A human self can enjoy that kind of freedom without representing any positive value or having any sense of direction in life. Yet in many democratic circles this purely negative freedom to do what one likes is the only freedom which means anything, a circumstance which is responsible for the confusion and inertia which mark democratic action to-day. A man who is free in any sense worthy of the name is free not merely *from* something; he is free *in* something or *for* something. He becomes free, paradoxically speaking, when he becomes linked in allegiance to something greater and more important than himself.

Whatever be the object of allegiance which a man may choose, his devotion to it will give him a sense of freedom, of release, of exhilaration. Such was the freedom of the Nazis, a kind of biological freedom which we commonly associate with pedigree stock. It is the freedom of the horse or hound which, knowing itself to be an elect favourite of its master, exults in his use of rein or whip. Such a person, laying all reflection aside, lives the exuberant freedom of the fanatic who brooks no restraint of any kind in the expression of his devotion. Freedom of this sort, while being psychologically real, has been the flail of our civilization.

But for man as a spiritual being, made in the image of his Maker, freedom that is freedom indeed is the fruit of allegiance that is given to God alone. A man is truly free not through allegiance to his autonomous self or to any aspect of it, nor yet when any finite reality, personal or institutional, racial or ideological, claims his devotion. He is free when he has made himself a willing captive of the Infinite, giving allegiance to God Himself. Spiritual freedom is captivity to the Divine by which a man, relating himself consciously to God's great scheme of things, becomes an obedient instrument of His will. " I would fain be to the Eternal Goodness what his own hand is to a man ", said the anonymous author of *Theologia Germanica*. " Man is created for true allegiance ", says the author of this great book which exercised so profound an influence upon Martin Luther, " and is bound of right to render it to God ". And again, " These men are in a state of freedom because they are living in pure submissiveness to the Eternal Goodness in the perfect freedom of fervent love." We might say, therefore, that while allegiance to a greater than one's self is necessary for freedom of any kind, conscious allegiance to God is the only allegiance which leads to perfect freedom. " Make me a captive, Lord, and then I shall be free." The man who becomes free in this sense can say with Luther, " A Christian man is the most free lord of all, subject to none. A Christian man is the most dutiful servant of all, subject to everyone." Of little value is freedom of religion as a natural or legal right if a man is, like young Augustine, the slave of his "own iron will".

But granting that only a truly religious man is fully free, what does freedom of religion mean? It means, first of all, *freedom to choose one's religion.* God has given to man the inalienable right of choice, whether to choose good or to choose evil. In making man free God took risks. The fact that man at the beginning chose wrongly does not alter God's attitude toward him as a sinner. He still leaves him sovereignly free to choose Heaven or Hell, God or the Devil, and requires that every human authority shall do likewise, leaving man free to make the ultimate spiritual choice without coercion.

When we look, however, at the world of men we discover people who are afraid of choosing. There is a profound insight in the declaration of the Grand Inquisitor, in Dostoïevski's famous tale,[3] that men do not really want freedom but rather bread and security. According to the Inquisitor men say, " Make us slaves, but sustain us." The dread of free choice and the tremendous responsibility which it entails lead multitudes of people to forgo the right to choose for themselves in the realm of spiritual ultimates. Such a situation obtains to-day. Aware of the innate craven fear in human nature to make an ultimate spiritual choice, certain religious and political leaders have proceeded upon the assumption that the range of human choice in matters of the spirit should be severely circumscribed in the interests of men themselves. Some argue that the choice should be limited to a choice between good things. " Liberty, correctly understood, is the right to choose between good things

[3] *The Brothers Karamazov.*

in order to develop the highest reaches of personality." So holds that distinguished Roman Catholic churchman, Father Fulton Sheen. In the famous Encyclical, *Immortale Dei*, Pope Leo XIII stated, " That liberty is truly genuine which, in regard to the individual, does not allow men to be the slaves of error and of passion, the worst of all masters." On the other hand, one of the most distinguished Roman Catholic laymen of recent times, the eminent historian, Lord Acton, thus expressed his conception of liberty: " By liberty I mean the assurance that every man shall be protected, doing what he believes his duty, against the influence of authority and majority custom and opinion."

Enforced loyalty destroys spiritual freedom. A religious loyalty has often been imposed upon people in the name of their best interests. A religion was prescribed to them to save them from the confusion of their thinking, the corruption of their practices, and the weakness of their moral decision. But whenever people have been forced to adopt religious practices against their will, the most devastating consequences have followed. One such consequence is hypocrisy, another is irreligion. Through the fear of sanctions, if they do not obey, or through the desire to gain some advantage if they do, people become hollow and insincere. They live with a lie in their soul which leads to the expression of falsehood in society as a whole. In the end, enforced religion always produces irreligion. Violent antagonism is engendered to all that the enforced religion has stood for. Contemporary Spain is one of the saddest examples in all history of what can happen to a great people when Church and State combine to maintain a religion which the majority of Spanish citizens no longer accept. Religious monopoly and the enforcement of religious beliefs and practices have invariably resulted in producing a spiritual situation that is totally inimical to the interests of religion and sinisterly productive of moral evil.

Where ultimate spiritual loyalty is concerned, the human soul must be left in utter freedom to choose the object of its devotion. It may choose wrongly, but those in power, whether in Church or State, who permit a wrong religious choice do no more than what God Himself has done and does. God rejects any kind of religious loyalty which is not in " spirit and in truth ". He would have human authorities follow His own practice, wooing but never ravishing the human soul to win its loyalty. Never does the Almighty violate the freedom of personality. The integrity of the human self is so precious in God's sight-that He takes measureless risks in His providential dealings with man.

Freedom to practise one's religion is a second element in religious freedom. Freedom of worship is not enough. For a man to be religiously free it is necessary not only that he should be free to worship God alone or with others in the form that appears to him to be most appropriate; it is also necessary that he should be free to propagate his faith among others. If he has a faith, he must be given liberty to share it with other people and to summon them to the religious beliefs and dedication which mean everything in his own life. Herein lies the issue between Christianity, on the one hand, and Islam and Soviet Russia on the other. It is the issue also between evangelical Christianity and the Roman Catholic Church. Russia allows freedom of worship for all Soviet citizens, but freedom of propaganda only for anti-religious movements. While the Roman Catholic Church invariably deals with religious freedom in terms of policy rather than in terms of principle, the official position of the Church is that where the Roman Catholic faith is professed by a majority of the citizens, the Church has a right to call upon the State to curb the propagandist activities of minority religious groups. The position of the Church of Rome is this: Roman Catholics, when they form a minority in a Protestant nation, have a right to expect that they shall be treated in accordance with Protestant principles of religious liberty; when Roman Catholics are in the majority, Protestants can claim no more than to be dealt with in accordance with Roman Catholic principles of religious liberty. One of these principles is that error, which means anything opposed to Roman Catholic doctrine, cannot claim the same rights as truth. The basic question between evangelicals and Roman Catholics on the subject of religious freedom thus relates to the status of error and the appropriate way of dealing with it. The major issue involved in freedom of religion to-day is not the issue with Islam or the Soviet Union; it is an internal issue within the Christian religion.

There are three possible attitudes which a dominant religious group may adopt with respect to ideas and people who are regarded as heretical. It may adopt an attitude of complete indifference; it may take up a repressive attitude; or it may seek by legitimate methods of persuasion to convert the heretics and so change their ideas. The only Christian attitude is the third. In God's world religious heretics have their sacred rights. They must be tolerated in a society, without any discriminatory measures being taken against them, provided that they and their ideas do not affect public order or basic morals. A fine example of the most successful method of handling heretics was illustrated by Timothy Dwight, the famous president of Yale College. In days when the Church was overwhelmingly strong in New England, Dwight, we are told, allowed young infidels at Yale to express themselves as blatantly as they chose. He then took issue with their ideas in public forum. Invariably it was the truth that prevailed.

But sincere Roman Catholics may reply that such an attitude towards religious heresy, when the Church is in a position to repress it through its influence with the secular power, fails to take into account the obligations imposed upon the Church by Jesus Christ. The problem of religious liberty cannot be dealt with, it is averred, in terms of reason and natural law alone. "It is our concept of the Church of Christ," says Father Murray with great truth, " that is the decisive element here." His contention is that the Church of Jesus Christ, because of its special relationship to the Church's Lord, is not free to allow religious error to propagate itself in the secular order. This is precisely the issue: What is the Christian Church and what authority does the Church have to deal in a summary way with religious heresy by calling in the secular power? This leads us to formulate some dispassionate reflections.

There are only two ways in which to deal with the conscientious conviction of the Roman Catholic

Church that it should treat religious heresy and heretics in a summary way when it has power to do so. One way is to see to it that the Church shall not obtain political power over the State so as to make the State an instrument of its will with respect to people and ideas that are obnoxious to it. The other way is to take issue with the premise upon which the Roman Church builds its claim to special status and authority. The time has come when in the interests of all concerned, and having regard to the future of Christianity in the world, the basic claims of the Roman Catholic Church should be challenged upon Biblical, historical, and theological grounds.

Our first reflection, accordingly, is this: There is no support in the New Testament or the early Christian centuries for the contention that the Christian Church is a single organization identical with the Roman Catholic Church, to which Jesus Christ has delegated His sovereign rights. Biblically speaking, the Church of Christ is essentially a fellowship rather than an organization. Historically speaking, the authority of the Christian Church as an organization lay in a general Council which sought to know the mind of Christ in all matters relating to Church policy. Jesus Christ continues to be the Lord of the Church as He is the Lord of the conscience. Whenever a hierarchy presumes to be the Church; whenever it alleges that, if it is in error, Christ is the cause of its error; whenever a supreme hierarch undertakes to be the vicegerent of the Almighty in such a way that God in heaven becomes the vicar of an ecclesiastical potentate on earth, then it is in order for many religious heretics to cry out with one of the greatest of Roman

Catholic laymen, Blaise Pascal, " To Thy tribunal, Lord Jesus, I appeal."

Second reflection: It is not true that the Church of Christ, whatever we may regard it to be, has a right to make the State an instrument of its will. The attempt upon the part of an ecclesiastical power to control the secular power gives birth to clericalism. " Clericalism," says one of the greatest of modern Spaniards, Salvador de Madariaga, " is an evil unknown in Protestant countries. Clericalism, though a disease of Catholic societies, is natural to them, being a diseased growth along the lines of their healthy development. It is therefore extremely difficult to attack clerical abuses without seeming to attack Catholic institutions, or even without being naturally drawn to attack them." Clericalism is the pursuit of political power by a religious hierarchy, carried on by secular methods and for purposes of social domination. It is painful to contemplate the sinister emergence of this phenomenon for the first time in American history. It will work its own disaster in Anglo-Saxon North America as it has already done in Iberian South America, but its onward march may leave much wreckage behind it. " Men never do evil so completely and cheerfully," said Pascal, " as when they do it from religious conviction." So far as Protestants are concerned they will act now, and we trust will ever act, in the spirit and words of William Penn: " We will oppose the Roman Catholic claims, but we will demand toleration for the Roman Catholic Church."

10

A THEOLOGICAL MEDITATION ON LATIN AMERICA

A RECENT PROLONGED JOURNEY THROUGH THIRTEEN Latin American lands moves me, in the spirit and within the purposes of this Review, to survey the vast continental area to the south of the United States. What is the spiritual significance of Latin America to-day? What are some of its ultimate spiritual facts?

A CONTINENT BEYOND BABEL

The necessity of making public addresses in Spanish to the most diverse audiences in all the countries visited made me impressively aware once again of the linguistic marvel of the Americas. Throughout the geographical immensity that stretches southward from the Mexican Gulf, one language, Spanish or Portuguese, is virtually all that is needed as a basis for human understanding and the communication of truth. Despite the existence of hundreds of dialects and indigenous tongues that are spoken by groups throughout this region, the knowledge of one or other of the two Iberian languages makes one, to all intents and purposes, a citizen of Latin America. Here Babel and the confusion of tongues are a smaller impediment to human understanding than in any similar area of the world. For Spanish, which is spoken in eighteen Latin American Republics, and Portuguese, which is spoken in Brazil, the largest country in the Western World, are so similar that there is no need of translation from one to the other.

Add a knowledge of English to that of Spanish or Portuguese and a simple bilingualism makes one a citizen of the Americas as a whole. If, therefore, the Western Hemisphere, extending from the tip of Alaska to Cape Horn, fails to achieve human understanding and spiritual solidarity, it will be one of the major tragedies in all history and one of the greatest shames in the annals of human relationship. What a linguistic contrast the American World Island offers to that of the other World Island, formed by Asia, Africa, and Europe, which in the recent movement of international affairs confronts the world of Columbus! What a human basis exists in the Americas for that "pure language", spoken of in the Bible, which is destined to transcend the historic problem of Babel!

Let me attempt to interpret Latin American spiritual reality in the contemporary period.

CAESAR

The form of political life under which the majority of Latin American countries have lived for the past century and a quarter might be characterized as "Democratic Caesarism". Each voting citizen has been interested in personalities more than in ideas, while he himself has been, by and large, a supreme individualist, a miniature Caesar. United corporate action has been invariably difficult, save upon those occasions when individuals were fused into a unity by some great passion. While the form of government, at least the name of government, has been democratic, some Caesar has generally held the reins. But never has any dictator been willing to admit that the government of which he was head was anything but a democracy. This political paradox has been maintained throughout the history of Latin America until you have the irony of Perón's Argentina, where, as the result of democratic elections, a constitutional dictator controls the country's destiny.

A famous Argentine sociologist once made the remark that Latin America as a whole had never succeeded in producing real democracy because its several peoples had never been brought into thrall to God or to any ultimate spiritual loyalty. Some writers have gone so far as to say that the Iberian soul, the most individualistic, as well as the most naturalistic, soul known to history, was never tamed. It has never ceased to be the patron, instead of the servant, of God and of every spiritual principle that challenged its ultimate loyalty. When Christianity came to Iberia it was de-Christianized and placed at the service of Iberian imperialism.

Democratic Caesarism of this traditional type explains the reason why Latin America has been throughout its political history a "rosary of craters in activity". In the course of the last thirty years all the twenty Latin American republics, save Columbia,[1] have passed through revolutions. What is much more significant is the fact that it was in Latin America that the new type of revolution which has been the chief characteristic and problem of the present revolutionary era had its first modern expression. The nineteenth century came to an end when the volcanic

[1] This was in 1947. Now Columbia is in the throes of political strife.

fires of the Mexican Revolution belched forth in 1910, to be followed by the same type of revolution in Turkey, China, Russia, and Germany. The violent protest of the aboriginal soul of Mexico presaged the fact that the ancient heritage of many a nation was to assert its right to shape the nation's destiny. This type of revolution is still under way in our time. In a world like ours if the peace settlement fails to do full justice to any nation's sense of heritage, it will seriously compromise every nation's destiny.

At the present moment the political life of Latin America holds a portent and a promise. The portent is Perón, the ruler of Argentina, who, inspired by the dream of reviving Colonial Spain under twentieth century conditions, seeks to force a totalitarian pattern upon public life and all the institutions of society. Perón would carry forward the tradition of Philip the Second and fulfil the frustrated destiny of the Spanish race in the Western world. The promise is Haya de la Torre, the chief of the APRA Party in Peru, a man who represents, in terms of to-day, the political ideal of Bolivar, namely, to constitute in the Americas a federation of free peoples. With his famous slogan, " No liberty without bread, no bread without liberty ",[1] Haya de la Torre is to-day the most intelligent and strongest figure in Latin American politics outside Argentina. What he stands for represents a bulwark against both Fascism and Communism in the Latin American political order. Perón was influenced by a group of fascistically minded Catholic clergy; Haya de la Torre was influenced by reading the Bible and by evangelical friends.

[1] *Ni libertad sin pan, ni pan sin libertad.*

Culture

The spirit, literature, and public institutions of Latin America have been predominantly secularistic in character. A positivistic philosophy of life, which has had no place for spiritual ultimates, has been the dominant traditional influence in the higher intellectual circles. Parisianism, a love of beauty, and a detached, critical attitude towards life have informed the spirit of thought. Latin America has also been, until recently, that part of the world where the divorce between religion and culture has been most complete. Religion has not been looked to as a luminous source of clear thinking, nor as a dynamic inspiration for human living.

In these last years, however, a cultural revolution of a very significant kind has begun. The Second World War cut off the continent from its traditional European sources of cultural influence and inspiration. In consequence, Latin American culture, for the first time in its history, finds itself orphaned and uprooted and thrown upon its own resources. An unprecedented note of spiritual agony can now be detected in Latin American thought. The conventional type of thinker was the very incarnation of the "balconized intellectual", a man who looked at life from the outside, without sharing in its agony, or being deeply concerned about his personal responsibility. He gloried in what he called "spiritual unrest" (*inquietud espiritual*); but such unrest was no more than a pose, a mood. Any thinker who identified himself with a great idea or a great cause was labelled a "sectarian" (*un sectario*). The great Spanish thinker Unamuno never ceased to inveigh against this type of intellectual.

He called him a *Don Juan de las Ideas,* that is, an ideological Don Juan, a man who made an idea a mistress of a night instead of the wife of a lifetime.

Now there is evidence, incipient though it may be, of thinkers who are in quest of great germinal ideas for which they may live and die. Men are beginning to think, as Unamuno put it, " with their flesh and bone ", as well as with their heads. Youth is in quest of truth in a fresh agony of pursuit. Faculties of Philosophy and Letters are being established for the first time in many Latin American universities. At no previous time in the intellectual history of Latin America has there been such a challenge to the introduction of the great luminous, dynamic concepts of the Christian religion. Never has a virile Christian theology, which looks at the life of man in the light of God, had a more challenging missionary task to perform than in the higher circles of Latin American thought to-day.

Another event of great cultural significance is that, for the first time in four centuries of Spanish culture, the Bible is being promoted by the ecclesiastical authorities, in some countries at least. The greatest single tragedy in the history of Latin American letters has been the virtually universal ignorance of the Bible that has existed on the part of all classes in those southern lands. The great library of Don Quixote, a historical symbol of the cultural universalsim which has been one of the glories of the Iberian race, did not contain a Bible. The old sea chest which Robinson Crusoe, true prototype of the English Puritans, salvaged from the wreck contained a Bible, which became the means of his conversion. The

Spanish knight and the shipwrecked sailor, the manorial library and the storm-tossed chest, are the prototypes, respectively, of the two historic types which have influenced the Western world. They are also parables of the two civilizations which live together in the Americas.

It is surely a fact which cannot be overlooked, because of its profound cultural significance and promise, that the first Latin American writer to win the Nobel Prize for Literature is the Chilean poetess, Gabriela Mistral, one of the very few writers in the history of Latin American literature to have been influenced by the Bible. This great Chilean authoress, the glory of Latin American womanhood, has publicly acknowledged that from early girlhood the Bible has been her companion.[2] Latin America's chief cultural need to-day is that the Bible should become known by its classes and its masses. The popular knowledge of the Book will constitute the most potent link of friendship and the most transforming medium of understanding between the Americas. Gabriela Mistral herself once remarked that her most significant contact with North America, which otherwise she found difficult to understand and appreciate, has been a common interest in the Bible.

Hence the significance of the new Roman Catholic interest in promoting the Bible. The first Spanish translation of the Scriptures from the original Hebrew and Greek, undertaken by Roman Catholic scholars and under the auspices of the Roman Catholic Church, was published only recently in Madrid.[3]

[2] See her tribute to the Bible in *Theology Today*, July 1946.
[3] *Sagrada Biblia, versión directa de las lenguas originales.* Biblioteca de Autores Cristianos, Madrid, 1944.

It is true that Catholic versions of the Bible in Spanish are cumbersome and expensive; the important thing is that at long last the Bible is being given an opportunity to enter into the stream of Latin American culture.

Still another feature of the cultural change that is operating in Latin America is that, for the first time in the history of inter-American relations, the United States begins to assume cultural significance in the minds of Latin American thinkers. Until quite recently representative Latin American men of letters, even those belonging to a country so traditionally friendly as Brazil, regarded the United States as a culturally barbarian land. We know, they said, that applied science has its chief home and its greatest vogue in this area of the world. We know that North Americans have a passion to buy up objects of art, first editions, rare manuscripts, and similar cultural rarities, in order to indulge their acquisitive spirit; but they have no real cultural interest in those things. Now, however, the outlook upon the cultural situation in the United States has totally changed. The presence of the new cultural attachés who form part of American embassies around the continent, libraries of American books in three representative countries of the Southern Continent, the coming to the United States of a large number of Latin American students, together with the fact of the continent's cultural uprootedness from Europe, are beginning to set the United States in a new cultural perspective.

But woe betide the future of inter-American relations should Latin America ever get the idea that culture is being promoted by its great northern neighbour for political reasons or with a political criterion. I am happily in a position to say, however, after close investigation, that the present official representatives of North American culture are men and women primarily interested in culture. They have been chosen for their cultural worth and not for the political service they might render. Nevertheless, the sooner the promotion of culture in the international sphere ceases to be a function of government and is delegated to religious organizations, and to politically disinterested institutions of learning, the better for the future of inter-American relations and the spiritual prospects of the Western world. As the situation now stands, dispassionate study of Latin American culture will reveal that the most significant cultural influence which the United States has exercised thus far upon Latin America has been mediated by American men and women, who, inspired by their Christian faith and their love of people, have lived their faith and represented their country's heritage in Latin American lands. In a word, Latin American testimony makes it clear that the evangelical missionary movement has been the most creative, as well as the most appreciated, cultural contribution that North America has yet made to its southern neighbours.

CHRIST

The Americas were baptized unto Jesus Christ; to the South by Iberian conquistadores, to the North by English Puritans. The great Genoese admiral who commanded the three "ships of Tarshish" that discovered the Western World, gloried in the name of Christopher. In that name, which means a "bearer of Christ", Columbus saw a prophetic expression of his chief mission in history.

Christ first came to Latin America with the conquering legions of Castile. In recent times statues of Christ, in marble or granite, have been reared on lofty eminences overlooking great cities. But the most characteristic Christ that Latin America has known and continues to know is still the traditional Spanish Christ, the Christ that Unamuno called "death's eternity, the immortalization of death". That Christ never truly lived in life and never truly rose from death. Even to-day in a great metropolis like Buenos Aires, when an ordinary citizen wants to say of somebody that he is a poor beggar, or a poor devil, he says he is a "poor Christ" (*un pobre Cristo*). For that reason the supreme religious task that waits to be done in Latin America is to reinterpret Jesus Christ to people who have never regarded Him as in any way significant for thought or life.

But according to clear evidence, a new day is breaking in Latin America's understanding of Christ. Not only has evangelical influence begun to make itself felt, not only is the traditional concept of Christ being purified and made more Christian within Roman Catholic circles, but leading laymen throughout the continent are beginning to discover for themselves the meaning of Jesus Christ. It was thrilling to find, in the course of a two-hours' conversation with one of Colombia's leading politicians, that the figure of Christ had become central in his outlook. It was equally thrilling to receive from the hands of the

THEOLOGICAL MEDITATION ON LATIN AMERICA

distinguished judge who presided in the large theatre meeting at which I spoke in São Paulo, Brazil, a new book entitled *Life of Christ*, written by the head of a Brazilian political party. The danger is that political *caudillos* and men of letters will claim Christ for their own particular programmes and ideas. The important thing is, however, that the time has come in Latin America when Jesus Christ is at length regarded as having some significance for the secular order. For thus far he has been a helpless prisoner, misrepresented and misunderstood, within an ecclesiastical order which, having ceased to be His mouthpiece and His servant, became His patron and promotor.

THE CHURCH

The Church which established itself in Latin America is a Church which never had a reformation. Yet in its membership in the sixteenth century were some very distinguished churchmen, belonging both to the clergy and the laity, who embraced evangelical ideas. Those men, however, were either exiled from Spain or suffered martyrdom for their evangelical faith. This Church, of which North American Catholics have become so critical in recent years and about whose work and outlook they have become so concerned, was the Church which exerted a dominating influence at the Council of Trent. It is the Church which produced the Jesuit Order. It is the Church which in its Spanish homeland has had throughout the centuries more clergy proportionately to the population, and fewer books written by the clergy in proportion to their numbers, than any Christian Church in the world. It is this Church which gave birth in the religious realm to what has become known in Spain as the " coalman's faith ", whose formula is the following: " ' What do you believe? ' a Spanish peasant was asked. He replied, ' I believe what the Church believes.' ' And what does the Church believe? ' ' The Church believes what I believe.' " This Hispanic Church, the contemporary Church of Franco and Perón, is the most devastating example which history provides of the tragedy of religious monopoly. Franco's Spain is its chief handiwork; Latin American Catholicism is its eldest daughter.

In Latin America to-day there is a very decided Roman Catholic renaissance. Its chief characteristic is a revived institutional loyalty, a new devotion to the Church as an institution and a new faith in its significance for society. This renaissance takes three distinct forms.

In some countries, as in Argentina, Colombia, and Mexico, the Roman Catholic renaissance is markedly *political* in character. The chief seat of political Catholicism in Latin America is Argentina. The Argentine Church, sixty per cent of whose clergy are Spanish born, represents Hispanic Catholicism in its most classical and terrible form. Its passion is power, power achieved by external pressure upon government, power over the institutions of society, power in the cultural order, power which relates itself to the armed forces of a nation. In Argentina recently several images of the Virgin located in different parts of the Republic were elevated to the rank of General. Each draws a general's salary, which is collected by the local ecclesiastical authorities. In July 1946 there took place in Bogota, the Colombian capital, one of the most imposing religious processions in the history of the country. The occasion was the coronation of the Virgin of Carmen. At midnight a High Mass was held in the great central square of the city, at which the Sacrament was distributed to eighty thousand people who thronged the square and the adjoining streets. The only group, however, which received the Sacrament as a group were the representatives of the Colombian army, navy, and air force. This is the classical form of Hispanic Catholicism, the Catholicism which crowns the Virgin and makes her a General, a patroness of armed might, the Catholicism which singles out the representatives of military power for special religious distinction. The fortunes of this type of Catholicism are, of course, hazardously bound up with the regime which happens to be in power. It is also the type of Catholicism that has invariably produced anti-clericalism and violent revolutionary reaction.

The Roman Catholic renaissance in the *intellectual* sphere is represented by groups of clergy and laity in several countries who are devoted to the teaching of St. Thomas Aquinas. They form part of the neo-Thomistic movement, whose high priest is the distinguished French Roman Catholic, Jacques Maritain. The neo-Thomistic movement, which has its finest expression and exerts its chief influence in Santiago, the Chilean capital, is interested in the formulation of a Catholic philosophy of life. Its promoters are concerned to help bewildered men and women to think through their intellectual problems.

This intellectual renaissance, which begins to influence men and women in all ranks of society, is contributing to bridge the historic and tragic gulf between religion, on the one hand, and life and thought, on the other. This movement, it need not surprise us to know, is anathema in the eyes of political Catholicism.

The third expression of the Roman Catholic renaissance in Latin America takes a *sociological* form. It represents the impact of North American Catholicism upon the religion of Latin America. It promotes a concern for social problems to which traditional Catholicism in Latin America gave no consideration whatever. Under its influence there have appeared in Costa Rica, for example, Catholic syndicates over against the regular workmen's syndicates. Here and there co-operatives are organized in city and rural areas. This particular expression of the Christian religion is violently opposed by the Catholicism regnant in some countries. In Colombia where the Church is a great land owner, even the Pope's Encyclicals appear in expurgated editions; those passages in which concern is expressed over certain social issues and a social sensitivity is inculated are carefully eliminated. To-day it is easier for a Protestant missionary from the United States to enter Colombia than it is for a Roman Catholic priest from the same country; for the Church in Colombia has vast vested interests in the present social order.

The Gospel

Over against the traditional form of Christianity in Latin America and the great Church whose representatives came from Spain and Portugal, the Evangelical Church is emerging in every republic. Its membership, scattered from the Rio Grande to the Magellan Straits, numbers some three million, to which should be added half a million German Lutherans in Southern Brazil. Evangelical Christianity is becoming a very potent and creative, as well as redemptive, movement in Latin America. It is entering upon its adolescence, upon a period of vigorous, lusty youth. Already in many lands some very distinguished personalities have emerged from the Protestant community — outstanding educators, preachers, soldiers, statesmen. The influence of the evangelical community in those countries is far out of proportion to its numerical size. In several republics, Brazil and Chile for example, missionaries have been decorated by the national government for their distinguished services to the nation. Streets, avenues, and public squares in several Latin American cities bear the names of distinguished members of the evangelical community, who during their lifetime had deeply impressed those communities. The outstanding film of Argentine production, and the one that proved most popular recently in Buenos Aires, was the life story of a remarkable English missionary, William Morris. Morris was an Anglican clergyman, who during a forty years' residence in Buenos Aires had educated, in an evangelical atmosphere, a hundred and fifty thousand Argentine boys and girls of the underprivileged class. When he died, the country's greatest newspapers, *La Prensa* and *La Nación* of Buenos Aires, told their readers that the Argentine saint had passed away. The film that enshrines the memory of

William Morris bears the significant title, " When the Roll is Called up Yonder ". That was the favourite hymn of the boys and girls in the Morris Schools. This great and gracious soul and the work he accomplished will belong forever to the spiritual tradition of Argentina.

But this meditation has become unduly long and must terminate at this point, to be resumed perchance in some future essay. Let this, however, be said in closing, and in the most emphatic terms : Evangelical Christianity is the most significant and transforming spiritual influence in Latin America to-day, and the movement whose progress will contribute more than any other to inter-American understanding.

11

MEXICAN MUSINGS

A BRIEF VISIT TO MEXICO, TOWARDS THE END OF last November, has provided the occasion to continue the theological meditation on Latin America which was promised in the preceding essay.

An Eastern Airlines' *Constellation* from Washington to Houston, Texas, a Pan-American DC-4 from Houston to Mexico City, and in twelve hours, between noon and midnight, with two long stops on the way, one had passed from the American to the Mexican capital. Five strenuous days of meetings followed in a great down-town church, which was thronged each evening by two thousand people. The meetings were held in celebration of the Diamond Jubilee of Presbyterianism in Mexico and were attended by delegates from many Latin American countries.

Mexico City was the scene, during the month of November, of two international gatherings. Two historic assemblies went on simultaneously in the Mexican mountains. A Christian Church, the fruit of missionary activity, celebrated its coming of age by organizing a General Assembly; the United Nations' Educational, Scientific, and Cultural Organization held its second world meeting. In the plane that brought me back to the United States I met acquaintances who had attended the meetings of the UNESCO in the old Aztec capital. We exchanged ideas on our respective gatherings. It was my conviction that a generation from now the religious event at which I had been privileged to be present would have more cultural significance for Mexico and Latin America as a whole than the academic festival of ideas which had been attended by my friends. For a cultural harvest can come forth only where religion has ploughed deep the fallow ground and where ideas soaked with tears and blood have been sown in the furrows.

This visit to Mexico, following thirty years of close association with the Latin American world, supplied increased evidence that evangelical Christianity is growing rapidly in Latin America and begins to be a significant factor in continental life. After seventy-five years of evangelical labour along a road where many martyrs laid down their lives, a Presbyterian Church exists in the Republic of Mexico, which has three Synods, nine Presbyteries, and fifty thousand members in full communion. There are in Mexico to-day, by a very conservative estimate, at least two hundred and fifty thousand evangelical Christians. In the State of Tabasco, where some fifteen years ago no religious services of any kind, Roman Catholic or Protestant, were permitted by law, there are now twenty thousand evangelicals. Evangelical ardour waxes throughout the Republic and glows southward over the whole Latin American continent. From the Rio Grande across the equator to the Magellan Straits, there is a throb of spiritual rebirth.

Several reflections took shape in the visitor's mind as he thought of this significant religious anniversary.

The first is this: *The new Mexican Church that has reached its majority illustrates a characteristic trend in Protestant missionary effort.* This Church is the indigenous creation of three evangelical Churches of the Reformed tradition. The Presbyterian Church in the United States of America; the Presbyterian Church in the United States, commonly called the Southern Presbyterian Church; and the Reformed Church in America, until lately known as the Dutch Reformed Church, have co-operated in Mexico, creating a single Presbyterian Church. That they should have done so is an example of the kind of cooperative effort which marks evangelical missionary progress in many parts of the world. It is an illustration of the significant fact that Church unity and the ecumenical movement began upon the mission field. Two branches of a Church which was rent in two by the American Civil War, and which in the homeland have not yet achieved union, have functioned in Mexico as one Church, as they have done also in Brazil, Korea, and Japan. Moreover, in the Presbyterian Church of Mexico, the Calvinism of Holland has been blended with the Calvinism of Scotch-Irish origin, to propagate the Gospel in the Mexican hills and valleys. Nothing is so unifying as common action on the road of Christian obedience. It is in missionary service, moving towards a common goal, that Christian Churches fulfil their destiny and have a right to be regarded as Churches of Jesus Christ.

In the creation of the new Church a cherished missionary ideal has been realized. It is the ideal that has inspired evangelical missionary activity throughout the world, namely, to bring to the birth self-supporting, self-governing, and self-propagating Churches. Such to-day is this new Church in Mexico. True also to the genius of the Christian religion when a missionary spirit drives it on, the Presbyterian Church of Mexico, free, responsible, and missionary-minded, seeks the comradeship of men and women belonging to the older parent Churches to help it carry forward its missionary programme. It is the growing reality of this holy partnership between the older and the younger Churches that is the new and reassuring thing on the world missionary front to-day. The missionary movement is no longer a thrust from the Churches of some lands across the political boundaries of other lands. It is a movement along a world front in which the representatives of the older and the younger Churches combine their forces in common missionary endeavour. The meaning of " foreign " and " national " begins to fade out, as brethren in Christ of different racial and national backgrounds bend their energies to the supreme task of making Jesus Christ known, loved, and obeyed. In this holy crusade, each crusader is assigned his place in the line, not according to the race or nation to which he belongs but according to his experience and gifts.

But there is something still more significant: *What took place in that Mexican Church in November 1947 represents the fulfulment of a Mexican dream.* In the middle of last century Benito Júarez, Mexico's most famous president, the Abraham Lincoln of his country, expressed this deep yearning of his heart: " Would that Protestantism became Mexicanized ". Protestantism is becoming Mexicanized, and the reality of its indigenization gives promise of a great flowering of the evangelical spirit, not only in Mexico, but throughout the Hispanic world. For Mexican Protestant Christians show the finest traits of a people in whom revolutionary fervour has always had a central place. A famous Chilean educator, José Galvez, once said to me, " You Protestants will never succeed in converting our Chilean folk. Your religion is too cold and too exclusively ethical. Our people can be moved only by incandescent passion. In the older days the Roman Catholic Church subjugated the masses of Chile with the glitter and awesomeness of its pageantry. People who live eternally on the borderline of misery need a religion that will transport them to a realm where they can forget their cruel lot and achieve spiritual victory over their circumstances and surroundings." The Presbyterian men and women whom I saw in Mexico, and the members of other denominations with whom I am acquainted, are moved by a kindling evangelical fervour which begins to capture the Mexican and the Latin-American soul. Every act of greatness in Spanish history has been the fruit of incandescent passion. Only a crusading approach by religion to the problems of life can profoundly move Latin-Americans, whether they have in their blood the classical surge of Spanish passion or the characteristic Indian inertia that awaits a spirit of flame. As one watched a great congregation of people in whom youth and age were bound together by a crusading determination, people aglow with evangelistic zeal, eager to fulfil all the responsibility involved in the universal priesthood of believers, one saw a new race in the making; one witnessed the spiritual life of a continent crossing a new threshold in its history.

But at this point a crucial question must be answered. What are the spiritual alternatives to evangelical Christianity in Mexico?

There are two. One alternative is *the cult of aesthetic nationalism*. In the Mexican Revolution of 1910 the pent up racial underworld erupted, setting the pace and tone for the modern revolutionary era. How rarely is it remembered, and how little its significance is pondered, that the Turkish, the Chinese, the Russian, the German, and the Japanese revolutions were all of the same essential type of which the Mexican Revolution was the prelude! In each instance historical, racial, and national forces belched forth from the volcanic underworld of a people's life. Mexico is a country where the conception of revolution has been idealized, where, until recently, the highest that could be said about anybody was that he was a "true revolutionary." The rediscovery and idealization of the national heritage produced a rich, aesthetic development. Everything Mexican was seen through rose-coloured glasses. Whatever could be acused of stifling the Mexican spirit or of tarnishing Mexican honour was banned. First the Roman Catholic Church, and then all religion, were for a time regarded as enemies of the Mexican spirit. The Mexican Revolution produced great art and engendered in all ranks of society a pervasive pride of race. It failed because it lacked a doctrine of man. Mexican man was idealized. He was told what his privileges were as a Mexican, but he was not told what his responsibilties were as a man. To-day, according to all evidence, and in the judgment of the most earnest Mexicans, the country is passing through a deep moral crisis. Never in the history of this great people was there less downright integrity in the classes and the masses. Mexico's cult of aesthetic nationalism is one more witness to the fact that man without God ceases to be man. The Mexican problem needs an evangelical solution.

The other alternative to evangelical religion is *the cult of a childless madonna*. The Virgin of Guadalupe, an Indian madonna without a child, is the national divinity of Mexico. F. S. C. Northrop, the Yale philosopher, in the study of Mexican culture which forms part of his book, *The Meeting of East and West*, draws attention to the fact that the national virgin of Mexico is a very unorthodox madonna. It was the policy of the early Roman Catholic missionaries in Mexico, especially the Jesuits, to relate Christian symbols to pagan sentiment. Pagan idols were placed behind Christian altars. By a marvellous stroke of ecclesiastical statesmanship, the story was propagated that on a hillside sacred to an Aztec goddess the Virgin Mary graciously appeared to a simple Mexican Indian. Northrop states the significance of the apparition with admirable insight: " Our Lady of Guadalupe is to the Indians not divine mediately, by virtue of being the purely earthly mother of Christ, but is, like the Aztec goddess of the spot in which her spirit first appeared, divine in her own right. Her image in the shrine supports this conclusion. For the churchmen in their artistry did not dare to tamper with the spontaneous movement of the

Indians' spirit by even attempting to insure the orthodoxy of the Virgin by placing a Christ-child in her arms. She appears in the shrine of the basilica of Guadalupe alone and in her own right."

There is no escaping the fact that to all intents and purposes the deity of Mexico's popular religion is a brown-coloured female figure who is divine in her own right. Jesus Christ plays a very secondary role in Mexican Catholicism, as He does in all Latin American Catholicism. Roman Catholic statesmanship to-day is eager to make the Virgin of Guadalupe the patroness of the Americas. In this effort an inner trend in the Roman system, especially in the Hispanic world, tends to come to maturity. So far as the temporal, historical order is concerned, the potent figure in the religious life of mankind is not Jesus Christ but the Virgin Mary who more and more appears without a Christ-child in her arms. Not only so, but the virile intrusion of the Risen Christ into the affairs of the Church is sternly guarded against. Homage is paid to the Redeemer of mankind, but He is communicated to the faithful in statuesque or eucharistic form, or as the Christ of the Sacred Heart whose cult Unamuno called the " grave of the Christian religion ". Jesus Christ functions under the strict control of Christian priests who mediate His grace and carry on His work. Despite all protestations to the contrary, whether in the Hispanic or the Anglo-Saxon world, the words which the Grand Inquisitor addressed to his Prisoner have become true : " We will carry on Thy work in Thy name; therefore depart."

12

THOUGHTS ON TRUTH AND UNITY

CHRISTIANS AND NON-CHRISTIANS ALIKE HAVE A common concern in these days. It is a concern which finds expression in two supreme and inseparable questions. One is the poignant question about truth; the other is the agonizing question about unity. Men realize, as they have never realized before, that they must reach an adequate interpretation of life. They realize, too, that they must learn to live harmoniously together. The reason is obvious. If thought fails to achieve clarity on life's deepest issues and life fails to have a binding quality, men are foredoomed to destruction.

Let us ponder these questions.

THE APPREHENSION OF TRUTH AND THE ACHIEVEMENT OF UNITY

The apprehension of truth and the achievement of unity are supreme human needs. This is our first reflection. Truth is needed for our darkness and unity for our disorder; for the minds of men are very confused and the relations between men are very chaotic.

The deep, encircling gloom cries out for light. The void, the unparalleled emptiness of our time, needs a brightness to fill it. In the souls of vanquished and victors alike there is an eerie emptiness. In Germany and Japan, of course, the prevailing Nihilism is more tragic, for, added to the absence of meaning and the lack of an ultimate source of truth, there is the hopelessness of utter impotency. Ever since the roseate hued bubbles born of messianic dreams were punctured, two great peoples have no centre for their gaze nor any inspiration for life as they face to-morrow.

But let no one suppose that the souls of the victors have all the brightness of meaning and the fullness of hope. A subtle, creeping Nihilism invades the American soul. Not many years ago a sensitive spirit wrote these words:

> Oh my country,
> It is Nothing that we must fear: the thought of Nothing:
> The sound of Nothing in our hearts like the hideous scream
> Of fire-engines in the streets at midnight:
> The belief in Nothing.

It is as true to-day as when T. S. Eliot wrote *The Wasteland* in the twenties of the century.

> We are the hollow men. We are the stuffed men.
> Headpiece filled with straw.

Much of American life continues to be "full of fancies and empty of meaning". Patterns of social life which many students of society blue-printed for our time are now but memories of great illusions, the fantasies of men who predicted the shape of things to come without taking account of the sinister forces that operate in human history.

When was there ever such an opportunity for Christian affirmation, for grasping the great Christian truths and flashing them in the abyss like flaming torches? Now is the time for the Christian doctrine of man, which proclaims that the human tragedy is due to the fact we men have been passing the " days of our years " off-centre. Contemporary man has not had a true perspective for his thinking, nor has his life revolved around God and God's purposes as the only true pivot of human existence. What an opportunity, also, to proclaim the Christian doctrine of God! Now is the moment to affirm God's righteousness and mercy, to proclaim that human off-centredness brings inevitable disorder in its train, to emphasize the fact that the life of mankind must be governed by everlasting law, to set in high relief that there can be no true peace in the arena of history save a peace upon whose cheek righteousness imprints its kiss, and above which mercy, which is over all God's works, erects its rainbow arch. Upon the one hand, man must be interpreted to himself; on the other hand, God and his ways must be interpreted to man. This can only be done by Christian doctrine. Therein lies one of the great tasks of Christian theology to-day.

But the Christian truth that is going to render this service must be truth that, besides being lit up with reality, has a lilt to it, a singing note. The only kind of doctrine that will solve the problem of the dark, empty void is doctrine that has a musical quality. It is " songs in the night " that we need, truth that will give to life not only meaning, but hope, and courage, and exultation. Truths that call for mere stoical resignation, or that undertake to clarify the mind without warming the heart, are not truths that can face the problem of our contemporary void with any chance of success.

Not less important is the achievement of unity. It is a plain platitude to say the world is out of joint, but the fact, platitude or not, is that it is more out of joint, and on a more universal scale, than ever before in human history. Physically the world is a unit. Spiritually and politically, it is a chaotic welter of atoms. The present disorder cannot long continue. In an atomic age unity must be achieved as a basic condition of the continuance of human life. Political unity which is an absolute necessity can come only in one of two ways. It can come as the result of a basis being agreed upon for a family of nations; or it can come as the result of conquest, that is to say, by the imposed will of one mighty power upon the other nations of mankind. Evidence multiplies at this moment that we are headed for a new imperial era in which the attempt is going to be made to establish a new Pax Romana by force, whatever that force may be.

In such a situation, the unity of the Christian Church takes on all the greater meaning. The Church of Jesus Christ, now represented in all the great areas of the world, must express ecumenical solidarity to face the unprecedented emptiness and the unparalleled disorder in human affairs. The Church must be a community where the Word of God gives light and where allegiance to the will of God gives harmony. But the Church must be interested in unity not merely because the human situation calls, as it never called before, for Christian solidarity; it must pursue unity in order to be itself. Unity in Christ is called for because such unity is the only true expression of the meaning of the Christian Church. If the Church is to glorify God, which means to make Him visible to men, it must manifest the unity of a corporate life and a common purpose.

A Sense of Truth Creates a Spirit of Unity

A second reflection is this. *A sense of truth creates a spirit of unity.* From one point of view, truth is something that we pursue and strive to grasp. From another point of view, it is something that pursues and grasps us. In the great humanistic tradition writers have vied with one another in describing the thrilling pursuit of truth, whose true nature ever lies beyond the vision of the mind and the grasp of the hand. Life could have no higher expression than the pursuit of truth as a bird, which, if ever it were captured, should be set at liberty again by the captor in order that life might continue to be a thrilling and perpetual quest of truth.

But such a sense of truth is totally inadequate, whether to express what truth is or to express what life demands when the full seriousness of the human situation breaks upon the mind. For truth is no mere object to be pursued; it is a subject which pursues us. It is something that grasps us, as well as something that we try to grasp. In a very profound and Biblical sense, truth is subjectivity. It is a seed that invades the soil of the spirit and germinates therein. It is a belt that girds the loins of the mind and braces it up for action. It is a fire that burns in the inner depths of the heart. It is a whip that lashes us forward. Such is Christian truth, truth in which thinking is done not merely with the mind but with the heart, which "also has its reasons". It is truth in which the very flesh and bone of man engage in agonizing thought. The true encounter with Truth takes place not in halcyon days when all is well and Truth's seekers pursue it under a bright sun as it flits from tree to tree like a bird or like a butterfly hops from flower to flower. The great encounter with Truth takes place in times of storm and fiery trial, when a sense of the tragic enters into life and men get ready for a great crusade. Then Truth is the starting-point from which the march begins, the light which gleams in the crusaders' eyes, the inspiration which glows in their hearts. Such, in a secular sense, was the sense of truth which gave Germans and Japanese their biological response to the mandate of their Fuehrer or their Emperor. They were like pedigree steeds whom the crack of a whip or the blare of a trumpet sent forth upon a mission with fanatical devotion. This same sense of truth it was that made Chinese Communists "gossip about their faith" in every market-place in China and carry on the propaganda which brought into being a formidable crusading fellowship in that ancient land.

Far be it from us to suggest that the Nazi, the Fascist, or the Communist outlook upon truth does it justice or is the sense of truth of which we stand in need. But this we do insist upon. The same sense of being possessed by absolute truth which made Germans and Japanese the tremendous crusaders we have known them to be in these last years is native to the Christian sense of truth. The only difference, and, of course, it is a decisive one, is this. Whereas

Germans and Japanese were possessed by finite realities to which they gave absolute religious allegiance, Christians are possessed by the God of Truth, who calls them and claims them and grasps them and inspires them in Jesus Christ the Lord. Christians when possessed of the Christian truth become propagandists, campaigners, crusaders, as Christians always have been in the great epochs of Christian history from New Testament times to the present. Their sense of truth fused them, as it has fused devotees of secular religions, into a crusading fellowship on the road of life. They achieved a dynamic unity as they moved forward together to proclaim their faith and to live it.

What the Christian Church needs to-day is the recovery and re-awakening of this sense of truth. Routine and complacency are too prevalent in our congregations. Let no smug, traditional churchman sneer at the Pentecostals or at the sects in general, or at those Churches that have a crusading sect consciousness. Our Churches must recover a sense of pilgrim companionship, of crusading fellowship. They must move toward the real frontiers of life where the decisive issues become clear and the decisive battles are won. The unity that Christian truth creates is a unity on the road, a unity made manifest in the devotion of a common commitment. Christian truth, therefore, is truth that we find and that finds us. When we grasp it, it should not be to encage it like the bird, but to unfurl it like a banner.

> Long, long ago the Truth was found,
> A company of men it bound.
> Grasp firmly then—that ancient Truth!

CHRISTIAN UNITY IS UNITY IN THE CHRISTIAN TRUTH

This would be our third reflection. *Christian unity is unity in the Christian truth.* Lest it should be said that we are here advocating a species of fanaticism or a code of behaviour only slightly distinguishable from that of those groups who have been largely responsible for the contemporary crisis, let this closing word be added. Christian truth and Christian unity are both unique and even paradoxical in character. It is most important that we clearly grasp the kind of unity which alone is consistent with Christian truth.

For Christians truth exists. No finite mind can ever formulate it fully, but its true nature can be grasped and its true pattern outlined. This is possible because Christian truth is the product of thought's application to what God has revealed concerning Himself and His redemptive purpose for mankind. The Christian proclaims in unmistakable terms that the works and words of the living God are true. He affirms that God has spoken in deed and in word. That being so, the Christian quest of truth is not the quest of something to be discovered; it is rather the interpretation of something that is given. When this given is examined it is found to be a Person. For the Christian the Word became flesh. Jesus Christ is the Truth. At the heart of the Christian religion is no mere luminous idea but a Person who is the Light of the World. Because this Person was perfect in word as well as in deed, Christians should think with clarity and live in goodness, for truth must ever be " in order to goodness ". Moreover, because Christian truth is personal truth it can only be fully expressed in persons and in the relations of persons. Thus it is in the Christian fellowship, and in the Christian fellowship alone, that Christian truth can be made manifest. It is only in the Church, in the Christian Church when it is truly the Church, that the fullness of God can be experienced.

Thus fellowship, community, is necessary for the expression of the Christian truth. There can be no Christian truth worthy of the name which does not express itself in Christian unity. As there can be no worthy Christian unity where Jesus Christ, the personal centre of unity, is not adored as Saviour and as Lord, so Christian truth is not perfectly expressed when it merely takes the form of subscription to a creedal basis. For love is itself an integral part of the truth and the truth must always be held in love. That being so, while there is no unity that is specically Christian whose centre is not Jesus Christ the Truth, there can be no truth which is fully Christian unless it has a place for love and the works of love as central and integral elements.

Certain consequences follow from this interpretation. It is most important, in a time marked by confusion and emptiness, that each Christian Church should earnestly strive to formulate a confessional basis which has all the richness of the Christian revelation. A luminous body of thought passionately held is necessary, if the Church is going to outthink contemporary confusion and provide a needed body of conviction for its own members. For Church members need an intelligent grasp of the Christian faith that they may satisfy their own intellectual needs and apply their faith in the diverse spheres of life where they carry on their work. There is positively no future for, nor should any encouragement be given to, a Church union in any part of the world which is not founded upon an adequate body of Christian conviction. It is of paramount importance that all Churches review the confessional statement of their faith and make sure that it is richly worthy of the Christian revelation and as luminous and strong as the contemporary confusion calls for.

It is equally imperative that the Christian Church pursue Christian unity in the fullest and richest sense. Christian unity inspired by and rooted in the Christian truth is unity in which the spirit of love must ever be regnant. No clarity in the mind can ever be a substitute for love in the heart. Passionate Christian conviction must always be accompanied by compassionate tolerance of those members of the Christian fellowship who hold to Jesus Christ the Head, but who cannot conscientiously see eye to eye with others upon certain important, though subsidiary, aspects of the faith. It will always, of course, be a problem to be passionate and yet compassionate, to have burning convictions and yet to be winsomely tolerant, to be uncompromisingly loyal to truth and yet to hold the truth in love, to do equal justice to orthodox thinking and holy living.

The more we ponder the specific nature of Christian truth and of Christian unity and their relationship to one another, the more the inner meaning of the Christian religion becomes clear and the more adequate is the standard provided for us to judge the life of the Christian Church. The reality of Christian fellowship is much more basic than the character of Church organization. The fellowship and all that it implies must ever be given a prior place to the organization and must always be regarded as more ultimate than the ecclesiastical structure. The saints in whom is the life of God and whose lives are lived in conformity with the will of God must always be regarded as more ultimate than the ecclesiastical structure. They are more ultimate and important than the theologians, the hierarchs, and the ecclesiastics. And even when the theologians, the hierarchs, and the ecclesiastics, because of differences between them which they conscientiously regard to be important, find it difficult to come together in unity, they must do so " as becometh saints ". Especially must they strive after unity when they enter the Christian Holy of Holies and sit down or kneel down together at the Table of the Lord. To refuse to admit to the Lord's Supper anyone who believes in Jesus Christ and who loves and follows the Saviour, to deprive him of the privilege of the Holy Communion in the name of any theological, hierarchical, or ecclesiastical principle, is a crime against the Body of Christ and a sin against the Holy Ghost. Evangelical catholicity, which is the only true catholicity, because it is founded upon and inspired by the Gospel, is a unity in Christ transcending the human differences in thought and rank and organization which the children of God have set up and which distinguish them from one another.

One closing reflection. Jesus Christ, because He is the source of Christian truth and the soul of Christian unity, is also the goal of Truth's quest and its living expression on life's road. Christian thinking and Christian living are thus a moving out from Christ toward Christ and a return from Christ to Christ. Christian truth is inexhaustible in its meaning and Christian unity is inexhaustible in its possibility. Lines which appear in the last section of T. S. Eliot's *Four Quartets* have a deep Christian message.

> We shall not cease from exploration
> And the end of all our exploring
> Will be to arrive where we started
> And know the place for the first time.

13

THE NEXT STEPS

THERE IS A UNIVERSAL QUESTION WHICH MEN ARE propounding to-day: " What are the next steps? " Statesmen ask, " What are the next steps to insure a righteous and stable international order? " Industrialists ask, " What next steps should be taken for the re-conversion of industry, that the maximum amount of employment may be provided and the demands of production met in the post-war era? " Educators ask, " What are the next steps in an enlightened programme for schools, colleges, and universities if youth are to be given an appreciation of true cultural values and equipped for living in the world of to-morrow? " The Christian Church asks, or should ask, " What are the next steps for the Church if it is to gain spiritual leadership in such a time as this, and prove that it is in very truth the Church, the Body of Christ? "

If the Church of Christ is going to play a worthy role to-day and to-morrow and rise to the height of its calling as the chief agent of God's Will in history, there are two decisive steps which Christians must take. First: they must abandon all by-paths. Second: they must believe adventurously in God.

The Abandonment of By-paths

Our situation in these days is closely akin to that of the two pilgrims in Bunyan's famous allegory. Christian and Hopeful had reached a sector of the road where travel became rough. They had but lately spent some days beside the River, regaled by its waters and by the fruit orchards that lined its banks. But now they were footsore and weary from the roughness of the terrain where " the river and the way for a time parted ". They longed for a smoother trail. So Christian, espying an attractive meadow on the left side of the road, looked over a stile that led to it from the highway and said to his companion, " Here is the easiest going." Over the stile, therefore, they went and into By-path Meadow in the hope that a little farther on the by-path might lead back to the main road. But, alas for their simplicity! Farther and farther they were led from the old path. In the meantime, a storm broke loose; darkness came down; swollen streams from the torrential rain made it impossible for them to retrace their steps that night to where they had left the highway. At dawn next day, huddled in a little shelter where they had passed the night, they woke to find themselves face to face with Giant Despair. The giant drove the frightened pilgrims to his castle which lay nearby, interned them in a dungeon and told them to commit suicide.

Perfect portrait of the life history of millions! Within the Christian Church and its precincts are hosts of people who insist that easy going must be an inseparable accompaniment of right living. They have left the Highway for alluring by-paths that branch

THE NEXT STEPS

from it. They have grown weary of a life that constantly involves the facing of unpleasant issues. They prefer to evade disagreeable travel and to seek easier going. But with what results? Their deviation from the path of Christian duty has led them through storm and tempest to the dungeon of Doubting Castle. Spiritually uprooted and homeless, nerve lost and faith gone, burning with remorse and chilled by despair, they fall a prey to all sorts of psychic woes. The suicide of the Austrian writer, Stefen Zweig, in the hospitable land of Brazil, amid the incomparable loveliness of Rio, and at the height of his fame, because he did not possess the spiritual resources necessary to enable him, a homeless wanderer, to make another adjustment to life—is an extreme case of a widespread despondency from which clergy and laity, churchmen and men of the world, suffer alike.

In such a case, men must clearly understand why they left the Highway and be penitent for their softness. A hankering after ease, smooth going as a standard of duty, pleasantness as a criterion of moral goodness, must be utterly rejected. All who profess Christ's name must accept the inexorable consequences of being Christian. Why should the dwindling membership of many a down-town church prefer a ghost-like existence to union with a neighbouring church in similar plight, in order that together they might present a vigorous Christian front to the new conditions that have changed the old environment? Why should a congregation that flees from a city into its suburbs to erect a new church in the more pleasant surroundings where most of its members now reside, abandon without any Christian witness the district where it was formerly located? Why should rivalries and prejudices in many a small town or rural area thwart church consolidation, and prevent advantage being taken of new methods of transportation whereby a single pastor can serve a larger parish than formerly? Because national prohibition was probably the wrong way in which to attempt a solution of the liquor problem, why should millions of Christian people to-day be ashamed even to express concern over the growing respectability of the cocktail party in church circles? Why should schemes of ecclesiastical union fail to establish racial equality in the projected new order? Why should sound doctrine, eloquent sermons, stately sanctuaries, exquisite services, alluring vestments, become, in a multitude of cases, pleasant substitutes for hard but inescapable tasks upon the road of Christian duty? And are we Christian people going to reconcile ourselves to the possibility that the aftermath of the Second World War may witness the canonization with pomp and splendour of gross injustices? The road to the City is straight and narrow and rough, and is skirted on either side by many a by-path that invites to less strenuous going. A craving for ease and comfort in every sphere of life, and an intense dislike to face unpleasantness, dog the steps and soften the wills of many modern pilgrims. Hence, Doubting Castle.

One recourse, and one only, offers an escape from the precincts of Despair's dwelling and a safe return to a crusading life. That recourse is prayer. After a night of prayer Christian remembered, just before daybreak, that he carried in his bosom a key called Promise which would open any lock in Doubting

Castle. With a spirit of exultation he put it to the proof. It worked. We must pray ourselves out of our confusion and gloom, and back to the Highway. Prayer, childlike, believing prayer; agonizing and importunate prayer; prayer which God answers by bringing to remembrance His everlasting Promise to restore the souls of all who trust Him, such prayer alone can rescue the Christian Church from its defeatist mood, and lead its members back from Doubting Castle and By-path Meadow to the rough, crusader's highway of God's will. The Voice addresses us: " Let thy path be towards the highway, even the way that thou wentest, turn again."

Adventurous Faith in God

But when the Highway is reached, what then? Thenceforth, *believe adventurously in God*. Have faith in Him. Take risks for Him. This is the second step.

The basic element in religious faith is, of course, what the Bible calls " The fear of the Lord ", that fear which " is the beginning of wisdom ". Reverence for God, which " the fear of the Lord " essentially means, is an attitude of the human spirit without which pure and creative living is impossible. A common reverence for God on the part of a people creates social solidarity and provides authoritative ethical norms, everything, in a word, which we associate with practical wisdom. The breakdown of religious faith darkens thought and confuses life. It destroys confidence and breaks the bonds of union. It removes the basis for brotherhood and saps moral energy. Educators do well in desiring, as many now do, that religious teaching be instituted in schools and colleges; for religious faith is the principal lamp of human culture and the chief cornerstone of national greatness. The nascent movement in both secular and religious education to restore theology to its rightful place, to make the great doctrines about God lenses through which to examine closely the realities of life and lamps to light up the darkness, are hopeful trends in contemporary culture.

The importance of religious faith as a light for learning and a foundation stone for living stands out vividly in the difference between the main course followed by secular culture in Latin America and in the United States. In Latin America religious faith never succeeded in becoming a creative influence in secular culture. When cultural institutions broke away from churchly influence they eliminated from academic life and thought all those things which were formerly associated with religion. Neither gowns nor hoods are worn in Latin American universities, for both would be accounted religious vestiges. The consequence has been that Latin American culture has never possessed a luminous Centre, nor has the Latin American spirit ever acknowledged a sovereign Lord.

Compare the heraldic emblems of two centres of culture, one in Argentina, the other in New England. On the arms of the ancient University of Cordova appears a condor with outstretched wings, and, written in Latin, the legend, *Ut Portet Nomen Meum Coram Gentibus* (" In order that it may carry my name before the nations "). The University exists and culture is pursued for self-glory. The emblem of

THE NEXT STEPS

Wellesley College, representative of a multitude of others in lands where the Christian religion has left a profound imprint on secular life, is *Non Ministrari Sed Ministrare* ("Not to be ministered unto but to minister"). Lowly service, not self-glory, is proclaimed as the goal of academic life and of all who go forth from those halls of learning.

But a religious spirit, however fully it may illumine thought and inspire life, falls far short of Christian faith. A further stage is reached in spiritual adventure when Jesus Christ becomes the central light for our interpretation of God, as well as the Master in allegiance to whom God is most truly served. The second element in religious faith might, therefore, be formulated thus: *Let life in its wholeness be linked to Jesus Christ.* Religion becomes Christian when Christ is at its centre. Christianity becomes evangelical when Christ is apprehended as the Saviour from sin and the Lord of life. Said Pascal, that most penetrating and mystical of Post-Reformation Christians in the famous document in which he transcribed the insights that came to him in a mystic rapture that proved a turning-point in his life: "He [God] is to be found only by the ways taught in the Gospel. . . . Renunciation, total and sweet. Total submission to Jesus Christ."

Let the Jesus of the Gospels never fade from spiritual perception as the pattern of moral grandeur. Let the Cross upon which the Saviour died turn ethical admiration into evangelical faith, and make the surrendered soul count all things but loss for His sake. Let the modern pilgrim not fail to take up as his personal cross whatever painful but inescapable thing meets him upon the road. And let him know, in so doing, that the cross which he lovingly carries for Christ's sake will become to him in the course of his pilgrimage " like wings to a bird, and like sails to a boat ". Above all, let him never lose the conviction that the Lord of his life shall finally triumph as the Lord of history, and that despite all appearances, life in its wholeness shall be redeemed by, and human relations fulfilled in, Jesus Christ the King.

But there is still a further step to be taken in the manifestation of Christian faith. Let Christians, in their corporate life as members of the Church, become a highway Fellowship. The life of the Christian community has been too long that of a wayside club. Even the achievement of unity and the joys of fellowship are not the goal of Christian living. The new sense of the Church, and allegiance to the Church Universal, have their subtle dangers. When the concerns of the Church and fellowship in the Church become ends in themselves, we have " churchism ", a deadly substitute for crusading action on the part of the Church. The Christian Church can never fulfil God's pattern for a true community, if it rests in the idea that God's will for and through the Church can be fulfilled in the perfection of family relations within the Community, even on a world-wide scale. No, the Church is truly the Church, not when it is perfecting its own life and achieving its own unity, but when both its life and its unity manifest themselves in churchly action upon the rugged Highway of God's Kingdom where the going is rough.

God intended His Church to be a Fellowship of the Road, whose members, knit together in joyous crusading comradeship, would proclaim the Glad Tidings and fulfil His other tasks. In its worship and its work let the Christian Church live upon the Road, as did the Lord and His Apostles, stopping the march only for intervals of rest and spiritual renewal. Let it succour the needy, bridge gulfs of division, throw down barriers, unmask hypocrisy, assault citadels of wickedness, face all the issues of thought and conduct, of life and death. And let none who are called by the Name and belong to the Fellowship succumb at any time to the allurement of a by-path and say, " Here is the easiest going ".

14

THE END IS THE BEGINNING

THE SAME AFTERNOON THAT THE FIRST GENERAL Assembly of the World Council of Churches came to a close in Amsterdam, two young people, one a student of the University of Prague, the other a student of a Dutch University, were engaged in animated conversation. The topic of discussion was whether the Assembly just concluded should be regarded as an end or as a beginning. A friend of the disputants who had been listening to the conversation injected the remark that the Assembly, truly understood, might be regarded as both end and beginning. And he made the further observation: In all things that are embraced in God's unfolding purpose, whether in the world, in the Church or in personal experience, the end is always the beginning.

This opinion would seem to enshrine an important truth. Where God is concerned, no end in a temporal sequence of happenings is ever a mere end; no achievement is ever an end in itself. For in the divine economy the end of an historical series is the beginning of a new march; the objective of a task concluded is that it becomes the terminus for a fresh start. The real importance of an historical event lies in the measure in which it gives birth to the new beginning which is hidden within it. In the Christian religion there is a pilgrim sense of beyondness whereby everything that God brings to pass points beyond itself.

St. Paul stressed this pilgrim sense of beyondness when he said: " Forgetting what lies behind and straining forward to what lies ahead . . ." (Phil. 3 : 13 R. S. V.). It is not that particular things belonging to the Christian past are unimportant; they are of timeless importance and should be remembered with gratitude. But their full importance and meaning will become manifest only as they become a new beginning and move onwards into to-morrow.

There are several things of crucial importance about which it can be said that the end is the beginning.

The End of the Christian Revelation is the Beginning of the Christian Church

As the human crisis deepens in our time, voices proclaim from high places of culture that man's state is hopeless. Solitary and alone he stands against the Darkness. For there is no God but only a Void, no cosmic purpose but only waste and welter. Christian faith is challenged to proclaim afresh that God and purpose both exist. Darkness there is, but it is the " darkness of God " within whose thick folds He dwells. Rarely so much as to-day has God been the hidden God who lives in the thick darkness. But out of the silence God has spoken and out of the darkness He has come. The everlasting Light shone in the darkness and the eternal Word became flesh in a Man. Ever clearer, ever dearer, ever more compelling, ever more relevant, the dramatic unity of truth that centres in the incarnation, life, teaching, death, resurrection, and ascension of Jesus Christ the Son of God, offers us to-day a luminous and a fighting faith. That core of truth is the foundation of God's order. Upon its once-for-allness falls the accent of eternity. It is the "still point of the turning world", the world that whirls in darkness.

Yet the revelation of God in Jesus Christ, for all its dramatic majesty and ultimate character, is an end which is also a beginning. What is that beginning? What is the supreme thing to which it gave birth? Aquinas' *Summa* and Calvin's *Institutes* were both born of it. The work of Rembrandt and of Bach, and of the great cathedral architects was inspired by it. Yet not for these was the revelation. When some people think of the supreme creations of the Christian religion they have in mind classical orthodoxies in thought or immortal embodiments in colour, tone, or form, of the influence of the Christian revelation. Let us eschew, however, the subtle thought that revelation has found its culminating expression in monuments of Christian culture. The Christian revelation shall continue to have its crowning significance not in great systems of thought or in masterpieces of art, but in the renewed lives of plain people. Not in scholars and connoisseurs, not in poets and artists, persons who were enthralled and transfigured by the grandeur of the revelation, but in a community of believers, "saints" in the New Testament sense, men and women who heard and obeyed the Gospel of God, and were recreated in Christ Jesus, did the revelation of God reach the end which was also the beginning. It is very important to remember this, lest we ever be tempted to give a dignity and ultimacy to Christian systems of theology and Christian cultural achievements which place their significance out of all perspective.

The Son of God became man, lived and died and rose again, and ascended into Heaven, that divinity might break into the lives of common people, that through faith in Jesus Christ, they might become sons of God and members of a new community, the Christian Church. Christian culture in all its expressions is dated in time. The Christian Church as the true bearer of history moves on through time. It is the Church, rather than any expression of Christian culture, that is the true instrument of God's glory, the medium through which he is made visible to men. " I have called thee by thy name, thou art mine." " This people have I formed for Myself, they shall show forth My praise." The revelation is consummated in living souls and in the life, work, and relations of living souls. And when at length the great role of the Church is completed, it will be through a survey of its life and history that the " principalities and powers in the heavenlies " will get their deepest insight into the manifold wisdom of God, into the innumerable aspects of the Divine unveiling. Therefore, let it be repeated, the Christian revelation is not for the sake of any achievement, however great, which makes that revelation a mere object of critical study, of devout expression, of theological formulation, or of pictorial art. It is supremely for the sake of Christian believers. Jesus Christ came that men might be saved, that the Church might be born, that through the Church the full splendour of the revelation might become manifest.

The End of the Christian Church is the Beginning of the Christian Mission

But the Christian Church, no more than the Christian revelation, can be regarded as an end in itself. The moment the Church begins to regard itself as an end, or to restrict its activities to a cloistered expression of its relationship to God in worship, it ceases to be in the fullest sense the Church. It becomes, instead, an idol and frustrates the unfolding purpose of God whereby He wills that all men everywhere should hear the word of the Gospel.

The Christian Church, to be truly the Church, must be a witnessing, as well as a worshipping, Church. The Church's constant temptation, to which alas it has often succumbed, in some eras of history and in some Christian communions more than others, is to exist exclusively for the worship of God. But no activity carried on in the sanctuary, whether in drab simplicity or amid the rapturous emotion created by the colour and tone of a great liturgical service, can make the Church the Church. It is paradoxical, but it is true, that the Church is not truly the Church if the expression of its life is limited to the love of God expressed in worship. What is still more paradoxical is that the Church is not truly the Church even if the worshippers love one another and succeed in constituting a true Christian community in which the relations between all its members are dictated by love. For the end of the Christian Church is not merely

THE END IS THE BEGINNING

that God should be worshipped and that the brethren should be loved. The worshipping community must carry the inspiration of worship beyond the precincts of the sanctuary, and the spirit of Christian love to the places where men live beyond the pale of the church and its privileges. The worship of God must pass into the work of God. The love of one's brethren must pass over into the love of one's neighbour, when one's neighbour does not happen to be one's brother in Christ.

When the Church is the Church, when the end is grasped as the beginning, the worship of God and the love of the brethren inspire Christian men and women to move into the " highways and hedges " where men live, and on to the roads that lead to the remotest outposts of human habitation. Evangelistic activity, missionary devotion, is the true end of churchly reality, that for which the Christian Church really exists in the world and by loyalty to which it will ultimately be judged. The Christian Church exists for what has hitherto been no more than a minority movement in the Church, namely the Christian mission. Bared feet that have stood in the holy ground of the sanctuary must be shod again with " the preparation of the Gospel of peace ", thereafter to tread the wilderness trails and penetrate the haunts of human need. The apprehension and experience of the Christian reality that is mediated through the Word and Sacraments are a prelude and preparation for the moment when the Christian witness tightens the belt of Truth around him, and unfurls Truth's manner for a great crusade.

Throughout the history of the Christian Church

the Christian mission, that is, the Church's missionary activity, has been a minority interest. Yet, even as a minority movement, it has been the greatest movement that history has known in the last two centuries. It was the Church's dedication to its world mission that made the First General Assembly of the World Council of Churches possible. The ecumenical Church of to-day, the Church which is co-extensive with the inhabited globe, is the child of the Christian missionary movement. One of the most significant things, perhaps the most significant thing, that the World Council of Churches did, was to commit itself to missionary activity as an essential aspect of the Church's life. Upon the official letterhead of the World Council one now reads, " The World Council of Churches, in association with The International Missionary Council." The Oxford Conference of 1937 said: " Let the Church be the Church." The Amsterdam Assembly said, in effect: the Church will be the Church only in the measure in which it takes its missionary calling seriously.

The End of the Christian Mission is the Beginning of the Missionary Church

For about two hundred years we have been accustomed to the Christian Church carrying on missions, missions within national territory, missions beyond the boundaries of the nation where the Church had its seat. We now come to a moment in the history of the Church and of the world when the Christian mission must give place to the missionary Church. More than in any century since the century of its birth, the

THE END IS THE BEGINNING

Christian Church stands to-day in an alien world, in a situation which is missionary in the most absolute sense. This situation can be met only if the Church as a whole becomes missionary. The ecumenical movement must not be allowed to degenerate into a movement of mere theological understanding and ecclesiastical *rapprochement*. Evangelistic activity and missionary fervour, even though expressions of a minority interest within the Church, have been the Church's glory. Both expansion and a growing desire for unity must mark the Church's life as a whole. The older and the younger Churches must be bound together in holy partnership to make Jesus Christ known, loved, and obeyed wherever the Christian Church is found or its influence felt.

To this end, the whole structure of the Church and all the institutions of the Church, must become more mobile than at any previous time in Christian history. The whole Church must advance with clear vision and sacrificial devotion upon the whole world front. This means something revolutionary. Not only must the Church advance into the geographical spaces where men live who have not heard the Gospel nor acknowledged the sway of Christ. Not only must Christianity make a missionary approach to the total cultural situation in the East and in the West. All who bear Christ's name must be prepared to be utterly Christian in all the spheres in which they move and in the several vocations in which their lives are spent. They must also strive that their secular calling shall make its own contribution to the purpose of God for human life. This can only be done if the laity are joined together with the clergy, to express in the life and thought of our time and in the spirit of the universal priesthood of all believers, all that it means to be " priests " of the living, redeeming God. Each Christian " priest " enjoys the full personal privilege of enjoying communion with God through Jesus Christ; each is equally responsible to lead other lives to offer themselves to God in joyful self-surrender.

But what beginning shall be the end of the missionary Church? Despite contemporary appearances, notwithstanding defeatist philosophies, for all the current distortions of Biblical apocalyptic, a missionary Church shall triumph in history. Through its crusading missionary action in the fellowship and through the might of the living Lord, the kingdoms of this world shall " become the kingdoms of our God and of His Christ ". The last conqueror shall be Jesus Christ and the organ of His triumph shall be the Church which is His Body. Christ's Gospel shall prevail in the earth; Christ's righteousness shall be done upon earth. Then shall the end come. *The end of the missionary Church shall be the beginning of the everlasting Kingdom.*

www.ingramcontent.com/pod-product-compliance
Lightning Source LLC
Chambersburg PA
CBHW062039220426
43662CB00010B/1562